W9-BAE-295

*Huebner School Series*

# SUPPLEMENT TO ELEVENTH EDITION OF FUNDAMENTALS OF INCOME TAXATION

THE
AMERICAN
COLLEGE PRESS

SS321-11

This publication is designed to provide accurate and authoritative information about the subject covered. While every precaution has been taken in the preparation of this material, the authors, and The American College assume no liability for damages resulting from the use of the information contained in this publication. The American College is not engaged in rendering legal, accounting, or other professional advice. If legal or other expert advice is required, the services of an appropriate professional should be sought.

© 2013 The American College Press
*The American College Press*
*All rights reserved*

Certified Chain of Custody
Product Line Contains At Least
20% Certified Forest Content
www.sfiprogram.org
SFI-00756

# SUPPLEMENT TO ELEVENTH EDITION OF FUNDAMENTALS OF INCOME TAXATION

This supplement to *Fundamentals of Income Taxation* contains self-test questions based on material in the textbook, as well as answers to the self-test questions and answers to the review questions that are in the textbook.

There is also a sample examination that tests your knowledge of the subject matter in the textbook, along with an answer key and explanations of each answer.

To guide you through *Fundamentals of Income Taxation* at a pace that best suits your learning style and time schedule, the supplement includes a chart that divides the material into 8-, 10-, and 12-week study plans.

# STUDY PLANS FOR 8, 10, AND 12 WEEKS

| 8-Week Plan | Material to Study |
| --- | --- |
| Week 1 | Chapters 1–4 |
| Week 2 | Chapters 5–6 |
| Week 3 | Chapters 7–8 |
| Week 4 | Chapters 9–10 |
| Week 5 | Chapters 11–12 |
| Week 6 | Chapters 13–15 |
| Week 7 | Chapters 16–18 |
| Week 8 | Chapters 19–20 |

| 10-Week Plan | Material to Study |
| --- | --- |
| Week 1 | Chapters 1–3 |
| Week 2 | Chapters 4–5 |
| Week 3 | Chapters 6–7 |
| Week 4 | Chapters 8–9 |
| Week 5 | Chapters 9–10 |
| Week 6 | Chapters 11–12 |
| Week 7 | Chapters 13–15 |
| Week 8 | Chapters 16–17 |
| Week 9 | Chapters 18–19 |
| Week 10 | Chapter 20 |

| 12-Week Plan | Material to Study |
| --- | --- |
| Week 1 | Chapters 1–2 |
| Week 2 | Chapters 3–4 |
| Week 3 | Chapters 5–6 |
| Week 4 | Chapter 7 |
| Week 5 | Chapters 8–9 |
| Week 6 | Chapters 9–10 |
| Week 7 | Chapters 11–12 |
| Week 8 | Chapter 13 |
| Week 9 | Chapters 14–15 |
| Week 10 | Chapters 16–17 |
| Week 11 | Chapters 18–19 |
| Week 12 | Chapter 20 |

# CONTENTS

# SELF-TEST QUESTIONS

## Chapter 1

*The bracketed number at the end of a question means that the question is based on that learning objective number; for example, a question followed by [3] is based on learning object 3.*

T (F)  1. The Standard Federal Tax Reporter is published by The Research Institute of America (RIA). [1]

(T) F  2. Federal Tax Articles is a comprehensive list of tax-related articles that are published in all types of professional journals. [2]

(T) F  3. One leading report for the latest tax developments is the Daily Tax Report. [3]

T (F)  4. RIA has an Internet product available by subscription called "Thomas." [3]

# Chapter 2

*The bracketed number at the end of a question means that the question is based on that learning objective number; for example, a question followed by [3] is based on learning object 3.*

T F    1. Congress was given the power by the original Constitution to lay and collect taxes on all income without apportionment among the states and without regard to census or enumeration. [1]

T F    2. Congress has the power to tax all income from whatever source derived, whether by corporations, individuals, or estates and trusts. [1]

T F    3. The statutory source of tax law today is the Internal Revenue Code of 1986, as amended. [1]

T F    4. The primary function of the income tax system is the regulatory function. [2]

T F    5. The Ways and Means Committee of the House of Representatives generally performs the initial functions related to the introduction of a tax bill. [3]

T F    6. The Internal Revenue Service is under the authority of Congress. [3]

T F    7. The only source of tax law today is the Internal Revenue Code. [3]

T F    8. A regulation may be declared invalid by the courts if the regulation is ambiguous and without persuasive force in determining the true construction of a statute. [3]

T F    9. Regulations are written by the Internal Revenue Service and serve as the official Treasury interpretation of the Internal Revenue Code. [3]

T F    10. Revenue rulings are written in response to a taxpayer's request for an administrative interpretation as to the validity of a prospective transaction. [3]

T F    11. After an initial IRS audit, the taxpayer will receive a letter stating the agent's recommendation and giving him or her 30 days to appeal from the determination of any assessed deficiency. [3]

T F    12. Taxpayers who bring their cases before the U.S. Tax Court are entitled to a jury trial if they desire. [3]

T F    13.   If a refund case is brought before the U.S. Court of Federal Claims and denied, the only avenue to appeal the decision lies with the U.S. Supreme Court. [3]

T F    14.   The IRS is bound by all lower court decisions with respect to tax cases. [3]

T F    15.   Acquiescence ("acq.") is the IRS's willingness to follow a decision in future similar cases. [3]

T F    16.   A taxpayer must first pay the amount of an assessed tax deficiency before filing suit in the U.S. District Court. [3]

T F    17.   The U.S. Court of Appeals in one region must follow the decisions of a U.S. Court of Appeals in another region. [3]

T F    18.   A taxpayer has a right to have a tax case reviewed by the U.S. Supreme Court. [3]

T F    19.   In taking a position on a tax issue, the IRS is not bound by decisions of the U.S. Supreme Court. [3]

# Chapter 3

*The bracketed number at the end of a question means that the question is based on that learning objective number; for example, a question followed by [3] is based on learning object 3.*

T F    1.  All income is includible in a taxpayer's gross income unless it is specifically excluded by the Code. [1]

T F    2.  Although there are 15 items listed in the Code that are specifically included in gross income, the definition is not limited to these specifically listed items. [1]

T F    3.  When a taxpayer receives a return of capital, the return of capital is subject to income tax. [1]

T F    4.  The release of an obligation to pay a debt generally results in taxable income to the debtor. [1]

T F    5.  Under the doctrine of constructive receipt, income becomes taxable in the year in which it is constructively received, although it may not actually be in the taxpayer's possession. [2]

T F    6.  The doctrine of constructive receipt determines whether or not a taxpayer has received a taxable economic benefit. [2]

T F    7.  When an employer lends an employee a company automobile for personal use, the employee has no income attributable to that use. [3]

T F    8.  When a taxpayer assigns income to another taxpayer, the burden of the income tax is shifted to the other individual. [4]

# Chapter 4

*The bracketed number at the end of a question means that the question is based on that learning objective number; for example, a question followed by [3] is based on learning object 3.*

T  F    1.   A deductible contribution to an IRA is an above-the-line deduction. [1]

T  F    2.   The standard deduction for all individual taxpayers is $3,800. [2]

T  F    3.   For tax years beginning in 2013, taxpayers with adjusted gross income over $250,000 are subject to an overall limitation on their itemized deductions. [2]

T  F    4.   A taxpayer who may be claimed as a dependent of another taxpayer will also be entitled to a personal exemption for himself or herself. [2]

T  F    5.   In order for an individual to be treated as a qualifying child of the taxpayer under the dependency exemption rules, that individual must not have provided more than half of his or her own support during the year. [2]

T  F    6.   A father can claim a dependency exemption for his 18-year-old married daughter who files a joint return with her spouse who has substantial income. [2]

T  F    7.   The phaseout of a deduction or a tax credit can increase the effective rate of tax that taxpayers actually pay. [2]

T  F    8.   A noncustodial parent may claim the child as a dependent if the custodial parent signs a written declaration agreeing not to claim the exemption for that year. [2]

T  F    9.   The lowest marginal rate of tax on ordinary income is currently 25 percent. [3]

T  F   10.   To file as a surviving spouse, a taxpayer must maintain a residence for a child of the taxpayer for whom he or she is entitled to a dependency exemption. [3]

T  F   11.   A taxpayer can qualify as a head of household by maintaining a parent in a nursing home. [3]

T  F   12.   Under the kiddie tax rules, net unearned income of a child under a specified age is taxed at the marginal rate of the child's parents. [4]

T  F     13.  The kiddie tax applies only to income from assets received from a child's parents.  [4]

T  F     14.  Corporations are generally required to file tax returns by April 15.  [5]

# Chapter 5

*The bracketed number at the end of a question means that the question is based on that learning objective number; for example, a question followed by [3] is based on learning object 3.*

T  F  1.  If alimony payments are deductible by one spouse under the alimony rules, the corresponding amount of income must be reported by the other spouse. [1]

T  F  2.  Payments of alimony may be made in either property or cash. [1]

T  F  3.  Payments constituting alimony made by a husband to a former spouse for her support are deductible by the husband and taxable to the wife. [1]

T  F  4.  Excess alimony payments attributable to the first year of a divorce will be included in the payer's taxable income for the third post-separation year. [1]

T  F  5.  The value of rent-free occupancy of a home by the former spouse and children of the taxpayer is deductible by the taxpayer as alimony and taxable to the former spouse as income. [1]

T  F  6.  When a former husband is obligated to pay child support for a minor child, he may deduct those amounts as alimony. [1]

T  F  7.  When a former husband names his wife revocable beneficiary of a life insurance policy on his life but retains ownership of the policy and pays the premiums, the value of the premiums is tax deductible by him and includible in the wife's income as additional alimony. [1]

T  F  8.  An annuity provides for a systematic liquidation of a sum of money, including both principal and interest, over a period of time. [2]

T  F  9.  The exclusion ratio for either an annuity or "partial annuity" is calculated by dividing the investment in the contract by the expected return under the contract. [2]

T  F  10.  The amount of each annuity payment is multiplied by the applicable exclusion ratio to determine the portion of the payment that is not taxable. [2]

T  F  11.  A refund feature in an annuity allows the annuitant to receive back his or her full investment in the contract before any portion of the annuity payments is taxed. [2]

T F 12. The actuarial value of a refund feature in a life annuity must be subtracted from the taxpayer's investment in the contract before the exclusion ratio can be computed. [2]

T F 13. For a taxpayer who owns a deferred annuity, all amounts withdrawn before the starting date are received tax free. [2]

T F 14. In general, an employer's contributions for employee group term insurance coverage are not deductible by the employer. [3]

T F 15. When group term life insurance is provided as part of an employer plan of group insurance, the cost of coverage up to $75,000 is not taxable to an insured employee. [3]

T F 16. A group life insurance plan might be found to be discriminatory in favor of key employees with regard to either eligibility or benefits. [3]

T F 17. A group insurance plan that covers fewer than 10 full-time employees must provide a flat amount of coverage to each employee. [3]

T F 18. Restricted stock is stock that a corporation sets aside for a key employee who cannot receive it before age 65, or age 55 if he or she takes early retirement. [4]

T F 19. An employee who has been given restricted stock is generally required to include the value of the stock in gross income when the restrictions are no longer in effect. [4]

T F 20. An employee who receives restricted stock may elect to have the value of the restricted property taxed immediately, even though the property is subject to a substantial risk of forfeiture. [4]

T F 21. When restricted property becomes taxable, the employee will recognize income to the extent of the fair market value of the property reduced by the amount the employee paid for the property, if any. [4]

# Chapter 6

*The bracketed number at the end of a question means that the question is based on that learning objective number; for example, a question followed by [3] is based on learning object 3.*

T F    1.   One essential element of a gift is that the donor be competent to make it. [1]

T F    2.   A gift of property must be in a form sufficient to vest legal title to the property in the donee. [1]

T F    3.   If a gift of property is excludible from taxation, the income generated by the gift will also be treated as a gift and received tax free by the donee. [1]

T F    4.   A bequest of a specific sum paid in three or fewer installments is generally not taxable as income. [1]

T F    5.   If the yield for a tax-exempt investment is 7 percent, the equivalent yield for a taxable investment is 10.77 percent if a taxpayer has a marginal income tax rate of 35 percent. [2]

T F    6.   Income received from nongovernmental purpose bonds is subject to the alternative minimum tax. [2]

T F    7.   Income from public purpose municipal bonds is exempt from federal income taxation. [2]

T F    8.   Interest on all U.S. Treasury obligations is tax exempt. [2]

T F    9.   Any gain realized on the sale of a tax-exempt municipal obligation is also tax exempt. [2]

T F  10.   Modified adjusted gross income, for purposes of determining the taxation of Social Security benefits, is generally defined as adjusted gross income plus tax-exempt interest income and the amount of deductible higher education expenses claimed by the taxpayer in determining AGI. [3]

T F  11.   The first-tier base amount for a married couple filing a joint return is $25,000 for purposes of determining the taxability of their Social Security benefits. [3]

T F  12.   Amounts received under workers' compensation acts are excludible from gross income. [4]

T  F  13. A taxpayer who personally purchases an individual disability income policy or major medical policy will not have to include the value of any benefits in income. [4]

T  F  14. A taxpayer who receives a jury award in a lawsuit for personal injuries of a physical nature can exclude the award from his or her gross income if no portion of the award is for punitive damages. [4]

T  F  15. If damages paid pursuant to a lawsuit represent lost wages, they will generally be excludible from the recipient-taxpayer's gross income. [4]

T  F  16. Benefits received from an employer-financed medical expense plan are generally included in an employee's gross income to the extent they provide reimbursement for the medical expenses of the employee's dependents. [4]

T  F  17. Employer-paid benefits for the loss of an arm, leg, or other bodily function are excludible from the gross income of the employee who receives the benefit. [4]

T  F  18. Benefits paid from qualified long-term care insurance contracts are excludible from gross income subject to certain limitations. [4]

T  F  19. Employer contributions to an accident and health plan are included in the gross income of the covered employees. [4]

T  F  20. Under the rules for a self-funded medical-reimbursement plan, the plan will be discriminatory in favor of highly compensated employees if it reimburses those employees for a larger portion of their medical expenses than other employees are reimbursed. [4]

T  F  21. Benefits received by a single parent under a qualified dependent-care assistance program are included in the taxpayer's gross income to the extent they exceed $2,500. [5]

# Chapter 7

*The bracketed number at the end of a question means that the question is based on that learning objective number; for example, a question followed by [3] is based on learning object 3.*

T  F    1.  A business expense need not be made at regular intervals in order to be considered ordinary and necessary. [1]

T  F    2.  Business expenditures are not deductible if they are illegal under state or federal law. [1]

T  F    3.  All business expenditures, including fines and penalties, are deductible. [1]

T  F    4.  Although ordinary and necessary business expenses are generally deductible, the expense must be reasonable to be deductible when it arises in the area of compensation. [1]

T  F    5.  The deduction for qualified higher education expenses is available regardless of the taxpayer's income. [1]

T  F    6.  A taxpayer has a choice between itemizing business transportation expenses or taking a standard mileage rate specified by the IRS. [1]

T  F    7.  Expenses for commuting are nondeductible. [1]

T  F    8.  A taxpayer who invited some of his business customers to his daughter's wedding may deduct the cost of the wedding as a business entertainment expense. [2]

T  F    9.  A taxpayer who invites a business client and spouse to a nightclub may deduct the expense, even if no business discussion took place before or after the nightclub visit. [2]

T  F    10.  Meals furnished to employees on business premises are deductible by the employer without regard to the 50 percent limitation. [2]

T  F    11.  Business expense deductions for tickets to entertainment events are limited to 50 percent of the face amount of the tickets and 100 percent of any premiums paid to a ticket agency. [2]

T  F    12.  Country club dues are deductible entertainment expenses if the use of the facility is primarily for furtherance of the taxpayer's business. [2]

T  F    13.  If a taxpayer does not keep records of the use of an entertainment facility, then for tax purposes the use of the facility will probably be treated as a personal expense. [2]

T  F    14.  If an entertainment expense is associated with the taxpayer's business, the taxpayer should record the place and time of the business discussion as well as the persons who were entertained and participated. [2]

T  F    15.  Expenses for tax advice are deductible as expenses for the production of income. [3]

T  F    16.  Business deductions are allowed for an office in the home whether or not the office is used exclusively for the taxpayer's business. [4]

T  F    17.  Home-office deductions (excluding mortgage interest expense and real estate taxes) may have the effect of creating a net loss from business activities. [4]

T  F    18.  A vacation home will not be treated as rental property if the home is used as a personal residence for a 30-day period during the year, and rented for 200 days during the year. [4]

T  F    19.  The 2 percent floor for itemized deductions applies to the deduction for annuity payments ceasing before the taxpayer's recovery of his investment. [5]

T  F    20.  Itemized deductions for gambling losses to the extent of gambling winnings are not subject to the 2 percent floor that applies to many types of miscellaneous deductions. [5]

# Chapter 8

*The bracketed number at the end of a question means that the question is based on that learning objective number; for example, a question followed by [3] is based on learning object 3.*

T  F    1. A taxpayer who owns stock that has declined in value may take a deduction for that loss. [1]

T  F    2. No deduction is allowed for a loss of expected income unrealized due to a shift in employment opportunities. [1]

T  F    3. When stock in a corporation becomes worthless, the stockholder may generally claim a deduction under the rules applicable to a sale or exchange of a capital asset. [1]

T  F    4. Gambling losses are generally deductible only to the extent of gambling gains. [1]

T  F    5. A taxpayer may take a casualty loss deduction for the value of a rare coin that he or she has mislaid. [1]

T  F    6. Individuals are allowed a deduction for personal losses in excess of a certain floor amount if they arise from either casualty or theft. [1]

T  F    7. A casualty loss that is not reimbursed will be deductible to the extent that it exceeds $100 on a single taxpayer's return or $200 for taxpayers filing jointly. [1]

T  F    8. If a car used for business is totally destroyed in an accident, the owner's deduction is equal to the car's adjusted basis if the fair market value of the car immediately before the accident was lower than its adjusted basis. [1]

T  F    9. A nonbusiness bad debt is treated as a short-term capital loss. [2]

T  F   10. Bad debts owed to a corporation may sometimes be characterized as nonbusiness bad debts for tax purposes. [2]

T  F   11. If a deduction for a bad debt resulted in a tax benefit to a taxpayer, the future unexpected repayment of the debt will be treated as income. [2]

T  F   12. The payment of a loan guarantee produces a business bad debt deduction only if the guarantor was conducting a business activity in making the guarantee. [2]

# Chapter 9

*The bracketed number at the end of a question means that the question is based on that learning objective number; for example, a question followed by [3] is based on learning object 3.*

T F   1. Capital expenditures include those made in acquiring or improving property that has a useful life of more than 1 year. [1]

T F   2. The cost of a capital expenditure is deductible in the year it is incurred. [1]

T F   3. Personal expenses, such as heat, electricity, and water, are deductible. [1]

T F   4. Premium payments on life insurance policies are generally deductible if paid by the policyowner-insured. [1]

T F   5. Medical expense deductions cannot exceed 50 percent of the taxpayer's medical care expenses for the year. [2]

T F   6. The cost of prescription drugs may be deducted as a medical expense. [2]

T F   7. A medical expense deduction is allowed for the cost of a weight-loss program for someone who is diagnosed with obesity. [2]

T F   8. Expenses for qualified long-term care services are deductible in *generally* the same manner as medical expenses. [3]

T F   9. Qualified long-term care insurance premiums are deductible in full as medical expenses regardless of their amounts. [3]

T F   10. Long-term care insurance cannot be offered through an employer's cafeteria plan. [3]

T F   11. Assessments for street, sidewalk, and other improvements levied against a personal residence are deductible as taxes. [4]

T F   12. Any joint owner of property who actually pays a deductible tax on the property may take the deduction for the payment. [4]

T F   13. Investment interest in excess of the taxpayer's net investment income can be carried forward and deducted in future years only to the extent of future net investment income. [5]

T  F      14.  A taxpayer may not deduct interest payments on loans secured by a personal residence to the extent that the principal amount of such loans exceeds the taxpayer's cost for the home. [5]

T  F      15.  Individual taxpayers may not deduct interest on credit card charges for the purchase of personal items. [5]

T  F      16.  If tax-exempt bonds are purchased with an investment loan, a deduction is not available for interest payments on the loan. [5]

T  F      17.  An individual taxpayer may generally deduct contributions to public charities in an amount up to 50 percent of adjusted gross income in the year of contribution. [6]

T  F      18.  Although civic associations, social clubs, chambers of commerce, and other business leagues are considered tax-exempt organizations, they are not considered qualified organizations under the charitable contribution rules and therefore gifts to these organizations are not deductible as charitable contributions. [6]

T  F      19.  Charitable contributions are allowed for gifts of "property" but not for gifts of services to the charity. [6]

T  F      20.  A taxpayer may deduct his or her $25 contribution for a church dinner that is worth $15. [6]

T  F      21.  Gifts made to foreign charities are deductible by the taxpayer provided that the taxpayer is a United States citizen. [6]

T  F      22.  A charity's rent-free occupancy of an office is deductible by the contributor at the fair market value of the occupancy. [6]

T  F      23.  Subject to certain exceptions, gifts of a remainder interest in property are not deductible unless the gift consists of the donor's entire interest in the property. [6]

T  F      24.  A corporation's charitable contributions are deductible in amounts up to 10 percent of corporate taxable income. [6]

T  F      25.  An individual making a charitable contribution to a qualified public charity may deduct contributions in an amount up to 100 percent of earned income. [6]

T F  26. When long-term capital-gain property is donated to a qualified public charity, the taxpayer's deduction may generally not exceed 30 percent of the taxpayer's adjusted gross income. [6]

T F  27. Gifts of tangible personal property are deductible at their fair market value, whether or not they are use-related for the organization's exempt purpose. [6]

T F  28. A charitable gift of a remainder interest is deductible when the gift is made in the form of an annuity trust, a unitrust, or a pooled-income fund. [6]

T F  29. A major benefit of a gift of life insurance to a charity is that the death benefit to the charity will be guaranteed, unless the policy lapses for nonpayment of premium. [6]

T F  30. The value of a charitable deduction for a gift of a premium-paying life insurance policy is the single premium that the insurer would charge for a policy of the same amount at the insured's attained age. [6]

# Chapter 10

*The bracketed number at the end of a question means that the question is based on that learning objective number; for example, a question followed by [3] is based on learning object 3.*

T  F   1. A "qualifying child" for purposes of the tax credit for children must be under the age of 19 at the end of the tax year. [1]

T  F   2. The amount of the tax credit for children (without regard to phaseout rules) is currently $1,000. [1]

T  F   3. "Qualified adoption expenses" for purposes of the adoption tax credit do not include costs associated with the adoption of a child of the taxpayer's spouse. [2]

T  F   4. The adoption credit must be claimed for the tax year following the year in which the expenses are paid, unless the adoption becomes final during or before the year the expenses are paid. [2]

T  F   5. A dependent-care credit is allowed for "eligible expenses" for the care of a "qualifying individual." [3]

T  F   6. The dependent-care credit is the same whether the working spouse has one or more children. [3]

T  F   7. Currently, the American opportunity tax credit may be claimed in amounts up to $3,000 per student per year. [4]

T  F   8. Both the Hope/American Opportunity Credit and lifetime education credits are subject to phaseout rules for taxpayers with modified adjusted gross income in excess of certain levels. [4]

# Chapter 11

*The bracketed number at the end of a question means that the question is based on that learning objective number; for example, a question followed by [3] is based on learning object 3.*

T  F    1.  Cost recovery allows the taxpayer to recover the cost of certain assets through tax deductions over a specified period. [1]

T  F    2.  Depreciation deductions for property are allowed only when the property is used in the taxpayer's trade or business or is held by the taxpayer for the production of income. [1]

T  F    3.  A mortgagee is allowed to take depreciation deductions on property with respect to the amount of the loan granted. [1]

T  F    4.  Land is a depreciable asset as long as the period of ownership by the taxpayer can be estimated. [1]

T  F    5.  A depreciation deduction for property placed in service before January 1981 was allowable under one of several acceptable depreciation methods. [2]

T  F    6.  Under the double-declining-balance method of depreciation, the annual amount of depreciation for an asset with a life of 5 years would be 40 percent of an asset's unrecovered cost. [2]

T  F    7.  A deduction for obsolescence may be taken when the taxpayer can predict with reasonable certainty that a particular asset will become obsolete at a fairly definite time in the future. [2]

T  F    8.  Obsolescence means that the asset has a normal economic life of 10 years, after which time it will be replaced by a similar, more modern asset used for the same purpose. [2]

T  F    9.  MACRS provides a cost recovery deduction for each year of a fixed recovery period. [3]

T  F  10.  Residential rental property placed in service this year is depreciated in the 27½-year class. [3]

T  F  11.  Nonresidential real estate is generally depreciated over a longer recovery period than residential real estate. [3]

T  F  12.  Automobiles purchased this year must be depreciated on a straight-line basis. [3]

T  F    13. For 5-year recovery period property placed in service this year, the recovery method is generally the double-declining-balance method with a later switch to the straight-line method. [3]

T  F    14. The half-year convention is used for all recovery classes of property. [3]

T  F    15. Under MACRS, the straight-line recovery method may be elected for property that is eligible for the declining-balance method. [3]

T  F    16. Lessees who make improvements to real property can be eligible for cost recovery with respect to the improvements. [3]

T  F    17. The Sec. 179 election generally applies to depreciable tangible personal property that is acquired and used in the taxpayer's trade or business or held for the production of income. [4]

T  F    18. If an election under Sec. 179 is made to expense the cost of a depreciable asset, the maximum amount that may be expensed is currently $500,000 for property placed in service in 2013 and $25,000 for property placed in service after 2013. [4]

T  F    19. The expensing election is available for property held for investment. [4]

T  F    20. The dollar limits applicable to luxury automobiles prevent them from ever being fully depreciated for tax purposes. [5]

T  F    21. Certain intangible assets acquired after August 10, 1993, are eligible for amortization over a fixed period. [5]

# Chapter 12

*The bracketed number at the end of a question means that the question is based on that learning objective number; for example, a question followed by [3] is based on learning object 3.*

T  F     1.  Generally, excess losses from a passive activity may not be used to offset nonpassive income for income tax purposes. [1]

T  F     2.  Under the passive activity loss rules, material participation means involvement in the actual operations of the activity on a regular, continuous, and substantial basis. [1]

T  F     3.  To qualify for the active participation exception to the passive activity loss rules, the taxpayer must own at least 20 percent of the rental real estate, measured by value. [1]

# Chapter 13

*The bracketed number at the end of a question means that the question is based on that learning objective number; for example, a question followed by [3] is based on learning object 3.*

T  F  1. Realized gain includes economic gain that a taxpayer obtains from the sale or exchange of property. [1]

T  F  2. Whenever a realization of gain or loss occurs, the transaction is taxable in that year. [1]

T  F  3. The "amount realized" on a sale of property is the same as the gain realized. [1]

T  F  4. It is necessary to determine the basis of property in order to calculate the amount of gain or loss on a sale or other disposition of the property. [1]

T  F  5. Losses on the sale of property are generally not deductible unless the transaction was in connection with a trade or business or an activity entered into for profit. [1]

T  F  6. When gain on property is not recognized but postponed to a future time, the property receives a stepped-up basis equal to its fair market value. [2]

T  F  7. The basis of property acquired by gift is determined by reference to the donor's basis in the same property. [2]

T  F  8. Property acquired as compensation for services has a basis equal to its fair market value at the time of acquisition. [2]

T  F  9. When a taxpayer acquires property subject to a mortgage loan, the taxpayer's basis in the property will be the value of his or her equity in the property. [2]

T  F  10. A taxpayer who inherits property from a decedent will assume the decedent's adjusted basis in the property. [2]

T  F  11. A person who makes a gift of appreciated property to a decedent within 1 year of death and then inherits that property from the decedent will be denied the stepped-up basis normally available for transfers of property passing at death. [2]

T  F  12. Death beneficiaries under nonqualified annuity contracts are generally not eligible for a basis step-up with respect to such contracts. [2]

T  F    13. Depreciation deductions result in a basis adjustment to the property that is depreciated. [2]

T  F    14. An exchange of General Motors stock valued at $15,000 for a General Motors auto valued at $15,000 is treated as a like-kind exchange that will allow taxation of gain to be postponed. [3]

T  F    15. Nontaxable exchanges occur when property is exchanged solely for other property of like kind. [3]

T  F    16. When property is exchanged for other like-kind property plus cash, the transaction is a fully nontaxable exchange and any gain is deferred to a future date. [3]

T  F    17. In a like-kind exchange, the basis of property received is determined by reference to the basis of the property given up, with adjustments to reflect recognition of gain or loss and the transfer of boot. [3]

T  F    18. An annuity contract may be exchanged for a life insurance contract in a tax-free exchange. [4]

T  F    19. Taxpayers who have resided in a nursing home for any period during the 5 years prior to the sale of a home may not exclude gain from the sale of the home. [5]

T  F    20. For purposes of the exclusion of gain from the sale of a personal residence, married taxpayers filing jointly may exclude up to $500,000 where both spouses meet the use requirement and one spouse meets the ownership requirement. [5]

T  F    21. A sale of stock receiving "wash sale" treatment assures a taxpayer that her harvested capital gains will be reduced by losses from any "wash sale." [6]

# Chapter 14

*The bracketed number at the end of a question means that the question is based on that learning objective number; for example, a question followed by [3] is based on learning object 3.*

T F   1.  A capital asset includes all property held by the taxpayer. [1]

T F   2.  Sales of capital assets held by individuals for more than 12 months result in long-term capital gains and/or losses. [2]

T F   3.  Sales of collectibles qualify for the lowest maximum tax rate on long-term capital gains of individuals. [2]

T F   4.  The portion of an individual's long-term capital gains from the sale of real estate that is attributable to unrecaptured depreciation is subject to a maximum tax rate of 25 percent. [2]

T F   5.  Individuals may deduct capital losses in full against capital gains. [2]

T F   6.  Individuals may deduct up to $5,000 of net capital losses per year against ordinary income. [2]

T F   7.  Excess capital losses that an individual cannot use in the current year can be carried forward and deducted in future years. [2]

T F   8.  Short-term capital gains and losses of individual taxpayers are netted together to determine the taxpayer's net short-term capital gain or loss. [2]

T F   9.  On the sale of depreciable real property held for more than 1 year and used in the taxpayer's trade or business, all gains and losses are treated as capital gains and losses. [3]

T F  10.  Sec. 1231 property used in a trade or business receives very preferential tax treatment; that is, gains from the sale of such property are capital gains while losses are fully deductible against ordinary income. [3]

T F  11.  A piece of art could be capital gain property, ordinary income property, or Sec. 1231 property, depending how a taxpayer uses the art. [4]

T F  12.  Two single taxpayers with identical amounts of MAGI over the "threshold amount" will always pay identical investment income tax. [5]

# Chapter 15

*The bracketed number at the end of a question means that the question is based on that learning objective number; for example, a question followed by [3] is based on learning object 3.*

T  F  1. Theft and casualty losses are not tax-preference items for purposes of the AMT. [1]

T  F  2. When computing the AMT, the standard deduction must be added back to taxable income by taxpayers who use it for regular tax purposes. [1]

T  F  3. Charitable contributions are generally allowable as itemized deductions in determining the AMT. [1]

T  F  4. Medical expenses of a 68-year-old taxpayer in excess of 7.5 percent of adjusted gross income are allowable in computing the AMT. [1]

T  F  5. Certain interest expenses are deductible in computing AMTI. [1]

T  F  6. Interest on nongovernmental purpose bonds issued after August 7, 1986, is generally a tax-preference item for purposes of the AMT. [1]

T  F  7. The exemption amount for purposes of calculating the AMT increases at higher income levels. [1]

T  F  8. The AMT rate for individual taxpayers is 20 percent. [1]

T  F  9. The AMT rate is the same for both individuals and corporations. [2]

T  F  10. A "small corporation" that is exempt from the AMT will later lose its exemption if its 3-year average gross receipts exceed $5 million. [2]

T  F  11. The ACE preference may subject corporations to the AMT on items that are not included in gross income for purposes of the regular income tax. [2]

T  F  12. C corporations may be subject to the AMT as a result of receiving life insurance proceeds. [2]

# Chapter 16

*The bracketed number at the end of a question means that the question is based on that learning objective number; for example, a question followed by [3] is based on learning object 3.*

T  F  1. Death benefits received under an annuity contract are tax free in the same manner as life insurance proceeds. [1]

T  F  2. Life insurance death benefits are generally excluded from the gross income of an individual beneficiary but are taxable income to a trust. [1]

T  F  3. A surviving spouse may exclude from income up to $1,000 of interest payable under any settlement option. [1]

T  F  4. Accelerated death benefits paid under a life insurance contract to a terminally ill insured are generally excludible from gross income as amounts paid by reason of death. [1]

T  F  5. Certain withdrawals from universal life policies that result in a reduction in the death benefit may be taxed on a last-in, first-out (LIFO) basis. [1]

T  F  6. When a life insurance policy is surrendered during the period that the contract is in force, the owner will be subject to income taxation on the amount received in excess of his or her cost basis. [1]

T  F  7. The portion of each installment of life insurance living benefits received income tax free under an installment option is found by dividing the investment in the contract by the expected total return. [1]

T  F  8. A policyowner who surrenders a level-premium whole life insurance policy and elects one of the installment options will be taxed under the annuity rules. [1]

T  F  9. When the primary beneficiary dies before receiving all installments under a fixed-period or fixed-amount option, the contingent beneficiary will be taxed on installment payments based on his or her life expectancy. [1]

T  F  10. Premium payments for life insurance generally constitute personal nondeductible expenses. [2]

T  F  11. The transfer-for-value rule provides that if an insured transfers a policy on his or her life to another for valuable consideration, the transferee will receive the death proceeds free of income tax. [3]

T  F    12. One exception to the transfer-for-value rule is a transfer from the insured to another shareholder of a corporation in which the insured is a shareholder or officer. [3]

T  F    13. If the transfer of a life insurance policy falls within one of the enumerated exceptions to the transfer-for-value rule, the entire death proceeds will be received income tax free by the beneficiary. [3]

T  F    14. Local law generally requires an insurable interest only at the time a life insurance policy is originally purchased. [3]

T  F    15. An individual who transfers a policy on his or her life to a qualified charity and continues to pay the premiums may deduct the amount of the premium payments each year as a charitable contribution only if the charity is the owner of the policy and has exclusive rights as owner. [3]

T  F    16. An employer who pays the premiums on an individual policy owned by an employee and insuring the employee's life may deduct these payments as additional compensation to the employee. [3]

T  F    17. Under a split-dollar life insurance plan, the covered employee receives the full value of the insurance coverage income tax free. [3]

T  F    18. A corporation may take a deduction for premium payments made for insurance on the life of an officer of the corporation if the beneficiary is the corporation. [4]

T  F    19. Interest on a life insurance policy loan of $50,000 may be deductible if the insured is a "key person" with respect to the taxpayer. [4]

T  F    20. Allowable interest deductions for loans from business-owned policies are now subject to limitations based upon the "Moody's" rate. [4]

T  F    21. Interest deductions for loans from business-owned single-premium life insurance policies are limited to $1,000 annually. [4]

# Chapter 17

*The bracketed number at the end of a question means that the question is based on that learning objective number; for example, a question followed by [3] is based on learning object 3.*

T  F     1.  The 10 percent penalty will apply to the total amount of any withdrawal from a MEC. [1]

T  F     2.  A life policy death benefit increase linked directly to the consumer price index will not be treated as a material change under the MEC rules. [2]

T  F     3.  All MECs issued by the same insurer to a policyowner during any calendar year will be treated as one policy for purposes of the MEC tax rules. [2]

# Chapter 18

*The bracketed number at the end of a question means that the question is based on that learning objective number; for example, a question followed by [3] is based on learning object 3.*

T F 1. A corporation is a business organization that possesses certain legal characteristics, such as limited liability, centralized management, transferability of interest, and continuity of life. [1]

T F 2. Limited liability means that it is only the officers of a corporation who are liable for the debts of the corporation. [1]

T F 3. A corporation is not legally dissolved on the death, disability, incapacity, or withdrawal of any of its owners. [1]

T F 4. A corporation is a separate taxable entity, distinct and apart from its owners. [1]

T F 5. One nontax advantage of corporate status is the ability to freely transfer ownership of the corporation. [1]

T F 6. The tax advantages of corporate status include the ability to deduct the cost of certain nontaxable fringe benefits for employees. [1]

T F 7. A corporation that elects to be taxed as an S corporation will have all income and losses passed through to its shareholders in a way similar to the partnership form of business. [2]

T F 8. An S corporation may not have more than 50 shareholders. [2]

T F 9. An S corporation election is a means of allowing start-up losses of a company to be deducted on the individual returns of its shareholders. [2]

T F 10. In all cases the incorporation of a partnership will result in current tax obligations to the partners on the transfer of their properties to the newly formed corporation. [3]

T F 11. One of the requirements for nonrecognition of gain on the formation of a new corporation is that the transfer of property must be solely in exchange for the corporation's own stock. [3]

T F 12. When a transferor to a new corporation receives stock plus cash, he or she will recognize gain to the extent of the lesser of the cash received or gain realized. [3]

T  F    13. The organizational expenses on the formation of a corporation are currently deductible in full. [3]

T  F    14. When a shareholder in a new corporation lends money to it, the corporation will receive a deduction for the interest paid on the indebtedness to the shareholder, provided that it is a valid obligation and the corporation is not too thinly capitalized. [3]

T  F    15. The highest corporate tax rate is 46 percent. [4]

T  F    16. The reasonableness test for the salary of a shareholder-employee is based on the highest 3 years' average salary of the shareholder-employee. [4]

T  F    17. The IRS permits a corporation to deduct without limit any salary paid to its officer-shareholders as long as the salary is specified in a written agreement. [4]

T  F    18. After 2009, the maximum deductible percentage of qualified production activities income is 9 percent. [4]

T  F    19. A corporation is allowed a charitable deduction for amounts contributed up to 50 percent of adjusted gross income. [4]

T  F    20. A corporation is entitled to exclude from gross income up to 60 percent of its net long-term capital-gain. [4]

T  F    21. For income tax purposes, corporation may deduct a maximum of 50 percent of any dividends received from other domestic corporations. [4]

T  F    22. Excess cash accumulated by a corporation to purchase key person life insurance is considered an unreasonable accumulation by the IRS and is subject to the accumulated-earnings tax. [5]

T  F    23. The personal-holding-company tax is imposed at a rate of 50 percent on "undistributed personal-holding-company income." [5]

T  F    24. A distribution of appreciated property by a corporation is treated for tax purposes as if the property had been sold at the time of the distribution. [5]

# Chapter 19

*The bracketed number at the end of a question means that the question is based on that learning objective number; for example, a question followed by [3] is based on learning object 3.*

T F 1. Generally, a distribution by a corporation to its shareholders with respect to the corporation's own stock is taxable as a dividend to the extent of the corporation's current and accumulated earnings and profits. [1]

T F 2. A dividend includes a return of paid-in capital to a shareholder. [1]

T F 3. The earnings and profits of a corporation for a given year are generally determined by using the corporation's taxable income as a starting point. [1]

T F 4. "Qualified" dividends are currently taxed to individuals at a maximum rate of 25 percent. [1]

T F 5. A distribution by a corporation can sometimes be taxable as a dividend even if the corporation has no current or accumulated earnings and profits. [1]

T F 6. When a corporation having no current or accumulated earnings and profits makes a distribution to its shareholders, the distribution is always taxed as a capital gain. [1]

T F 7. A pro rata redemption among all shareholders of a corporation will not be taxed as a capital transaction. [2]

T F 8. Redemptions in which the shareholder's percentage of ownership in the corporation is not materially affected are taxed as capital transactions. [2]

T F 9. A corporation's redemption of its own stock will be treated as a capital transaction if the distribution is not essentially equivalent to a dividend. [2]

T F 10. A redemption of stock that is substantially disproportionate will not be taxed as a dividend to its shareholders. [2]

T F 11. One requirement for a substantially disproportionate redemption is that immediately after the redemption, the shareholder must own less than one-half of the total combined voting power of all classes of outstanding stock entitled to vote. [2]

T F    12. One requirement for a substantially disproportionate redemption is that the redeemed shareholder's percentage of ownership or voting stock after the redemption must be less than 80 percent of his or her percentage ownership of voting stock before the redemption. [2]

T F    13. Under the 80 percent test, the reduction in outstanding shares resulting from the redemption is ignored. [2]

T F    14. Both the number of shares owned by the redeemed shareholder and the total number of shares outstanding will be affected by a redemption. [2]

T F    15. A distribution in complete redemption of stock is taxed as a dividend. [2]

T F    16. Under the family attribution rules, an individual is considered to own all the stock owned by his or her spouse, parents, children, and grandchildren, but not that of his or her grandparents. [3]

T F    17. The attribution rules do not extend to stock owned directly or indirectly by or for a partnership or estate. [3]

T F    18. A shareholder in a family corporation may avoid the family attribution rules if all the stock he or she actually owns is redeemed and certain other requirements are met. [4]

T F    19. Stock owned by a deceased shareholder may be redeemed to pay federal estate taxes and taxed as an exchange only if the value of the decedent's stock exceeds 65 percent of his or her adjusted gross estate. [4]

T F    20. A Sec. 303 redemption will be allowed to the extent that the proceeds from the redemption do not exceed a decedent's basis in stock. [4]

# Chapter 20

*The bracketed number at the end of a question means that the question is based on that learning objective number; for example, a question followed by [3] is based on learning object 3.*

T  F    1. Business organizations that are unincorporated under state law may generally choose whether to be taxed as partnerships or corporations. [1]

T  F    2. A limited liability company has the corporate characteristic of limited liability but may be taxed as a partnership. [1]

T  F    3. Profits earned by a partnership are taxed twice: once to the partnership itself and also to its owners. [1]

T  F    4. Partners in a partnership may deduct their shares of the partnership's net loss on their individual tax returns, assuming sufficient basis in the partnership interest. [1]

T  F    5. The aggregate theory and the entity theory are two theories of partnership taxation used in tax law relating to partnerships and their partners. [1]

T  F    6. When a partner contributes appreciated assets to a partnership, he or she recognizes gain on the transfer. [2]

T  F    7. A partnership files its own partnership return and pays partnership income taxes. [2]

T  F    8. A partner's distributive share of items of partnership income or loss is included in his or her personal tax return. [2]

T  F    9. A partner's distributive share is generally determined in accordance with the partnership agreement. [2]

T  F   10. If a partner lends money to his or her partnership as an outsider—namely, not as a partner—then the basis of his or her partnership interest is not affected. [2]

T  F   11. The basis of a contributing partner's partnership interest is generally the amount of cash contributed plus the adjusted basis of the property he or she contributes to the partnership. [2]

T  F   12. Taxable income may be realized by a contributing partner where services are contributed for an interest in the partnership capital. [2]

T  F    13.  A retiring partner's share of the gain attributable to inventory is treated as ordinary income when the partnership liquidates the retiring partner's interest. [3]

T  F    14.  Upon the liquidation of an interest in a service partnership, payments for goodwill are treated as capital gain regardless of whether they are mentioned as such in the partnership agreement. [3]

T  F    15.  A manufacturing partnership can deduct payments for unrealized receivables when liquidating a retiring partner's interest. [3]

T  F    16.  A limited partner in a limited partnership has liability only to the extent of his or her financial contribution to the partnership. [4]

T  F    17.  Generally, limited partners are limited in authority. [4]

T  F    18.  A family partnership is recognized as a partnership for tax purposes if the partnership arrangement has economic reality. [4]

T  F    19.  In a family partnership that is capital intensive, a donee of a partnership interest will be taxed on his or her share of partnership income even if the donor retains control over the exercise of the donee's partnership interest. [4]

T  F    20.  In a family partnership where capital is not a material income-producing factor, a donee of a partnership interest must contribute services in order to be treated as a partner for tax purposes. [4]

# ANSWERS TO REVIEW AND SELF-TEST QUESTIONS

## Chapter 1

## Answers to Review Questions

1. A primary RIA service is the Federal Tax Coordinator, and for CCH, the Standard Federal Tax Reporter.

2. Printed versions of each consist of multivolume loose-leaf sets with updates provided regularly in the form of replacement sheets or add-ons. Each also includes Code sections and the current regulations promulgated thereunder. In addition, each includes explanatory material and case citations or annotations that summarize court decisions and provide reference to the full text of opinions related to a particular subject or issue. Online versions of both services are also available.

   RIA's Federal Tax Coordinator offers a Practice Aids volume, which contains tax ideas along with reprints of IRS audit manuals. It also provides proposed regulations, reprints of recent revenue rulings, revenue procedures, and revenue bulletins.

   The CCH Standard Federal Tax Reporter service, on the other hand, offers more verbatim reprints of various elements of primary-source tax law and more extensive annotations of court decisions. In addition, it offers a two-volume Citator that shows where each listed decision has been cited and discussed in later court decisions.

3. Each of the major tax services publishes verbatim versions of new tax legislation and accompanying legislative history, explanatory material, and analysis. Major accounting firms also publish summaries of each new piece of federal tax legislation both in printed form and on the Internet. In addition, various government Web sites, such as the "Thomas" site, also provide text of new legislation, committee reports, and related material.

   One leading report for the latest tax developments is the Daily Tax Report published by the Bureau of National Affairs (BNA). Another is the CCH Tax Tracker News. Both CCH and RIA have Internet products that provide quick access to the latest developments in all areas of tax law.

## Self-Test Answers for Chapter 1

1. False. The Standard Federal Tax Reporter is published by CCH.
2. True.
3. True.
4. False. RIA has an Internet product called "Checkpoint."

# Chapter 2

## Answers to Review Questions

1.  The 16th Amendment, ratified in 1913, gives Congress the power to impose and collect taxes on all forms of income without apportionment among the states and without regard to census or enumeration. The all-encompassing language, "income, from whatever source derived," gave Congress authority to pass the first broad income tax law known as the Revenue Act of 1913.

2.  Answers:

    a.  The entire federal tax law was codified in 1939 as the Internal Revenue Code of 1939. The present statutory source of our income tax law is the Internal Revenue Code of 1986, as amended.
    b.  The Internal Revenue Code contains our income tax statutes. It must be followed by all taxpayers unless a provision is declared unconstitutional. The Code is subject to much interpretation but can be amended only by an act of Congress. The present Code is revised and updated almost annually. Parts of it can be amended or repealed through the passage of tax bills.

3.  The four functions of the income tax system are the revenue-producing function, the economic function, the social function, and the regulatory function. The purpose of the revenue-producing function is to supply money for the administration and operation of the federal government. The economic function plays an important role in the management of the nation's economy. The social function's purpose is to effectuate government policy. And the purpose of the regulatory function is to discourage socially undesirable activities by taxing them.

4.  Greater taxes result in lower spending by consumers. By reducing consumer spending without increasing governmental expenditures, the income tax system helps curb inflationary pressures. Conversely, the use of tax incentives or lower tax rates leaves consumers with more cash that, in turn, translates into increased spending, saving, and investment. The hoped-for result is an increase in the national product that will increase the demand for new workers and hence reduce unemployment. Thus the tax system can prevent or reduce the impact of recessions.

5.  A revenue bill becomes law, in most cases, through the following process:

    *   The bill is written by or referred to the House Ways and Means Committee.
    *   The committee conducts hearings on the bill and then sends the amended bill with the committee's report to the House for adoption.
    *   The adopted bill is then sent to the Senate Finance Committee for study and amendments.
    *   The amended bill is then forwarded to the Senate for passage.
    *   A joint conference committee consisting of members from both the House and Senate develops a compromise version of the bill if material differences exist between the two versions.
    *   If the compromise version passes both the House and Senate, the bill is then sent to the President for his signature or veto.
    *   If the bill is vetoed, a two-thirds majority of both the House and Senate can revive the bill and make it law over the President's veto.

6.  The president is the chief of the executive branch of the federal government. The Constitution gives him or her the duty to enforce the collection of taxes. The president has delegated this duty to the Department of the Treasury, which in turn has delegated this

responsibility to the Internal Revenue Service, one of its subdivisions. The Department of the Treasury also has the power, granted by Congress, to enact regulations to interpret the Code.

7. The function of a regulation is to give a fuller explanation and interpretation of an Internal Revenue Code section. The Code specifically provides that the Secretary of the Treasury or his or her delegate will prescribe these regulations.

8. Answers:

   a. The IRS does not consider itself bound (beyond the particular case) where a regulation is held invalid by any court lower than the Supreme Court, although it now conforms to circuit (appeals) court decisions for the taxpayer's circuit. Therefore, if a regulation is held invalid by a lower (trial) court, the IRS can and will continue to enforce it against other taxpayers.

   b. If a regulation is held invalid by the Supreme Court, the IRS is bound by the decision for all cases and must cease enforcement of the regulation.

9. Answers:

   a. Revenue rulings are based on a stated set of facts that usually involve a problem common to a number of taxpayers. They are binding on the IRS, which follows them in the handling of issues arising in particular cases.

   b. Revenue rulings are issued by the IRS and are published in a weekly bulletin called the Internal Revenue Bulletin. The first number following "Rev. Rul." is the year it was issued. The second number is in numerical sequence, denoting the order in which it was issued.

10. Private rulings arise when a taxpayer requests an administrative interpretation on a prospective transaction or on completed transactions that are not involved in returns already filed. Private rulings are personal to the taxpayer but, nonetheless, have been made available to the public in recent years and are now published. Even though published, however, they still may not be claimed by another taxpayer as a precedent.

    Revenue rulings, on the other hand, usually involve a problem common to a number of taxpayers instead of just one. They are binding on officials of the IRS and may be relied upon by taxpayers who have cases with facts and circumstances substantially the same as those in the rulings.

11. Revenue procedures describe internal practices and procedures within the IRS and are published in the Internal Revenue Bulletin. New revenue procedures are usually prompted by changes in techniques and administrative procedures used by the IRS.

12. Determination letters are written by IRS officials within specific operating divisions. They are written in regard to various transactions to be reflected on returns that will be filed by various types of taxpayers and organizations. They are issued only if the answer to the question presented is covered specifically by statute, Treasury decision, or regulation, or specifically by a court decision or ruling opinion published in the Internal Revenue Bulletin. Determination letters contrast with revenue rulings in that such letters are never issued about unclear points of law.

13. Answers:

    a. If a taxpayer disagrees with the IRS concerning the amount of tax owed, he or she may request a hearing before the IRS Appeals organization. While the dispute with IRS is being considered, the appeals officers are not permitted to engage in substantive discussions regarding the specific case with other IRS officials in the absence of the taxpayer or his or her representative. In addition, the taxpayer may request that the issue be referred to the National Office staff for technical advice if there is a lack of uniformity in the disposition of the issue or if the issue is significantly complex or unique. Dispute resolution methods in Appeals now also include mediation and arbitration.

    b. If the taxpayer and the IRS are not able to resolve their conflict in Appeals, statutory notice of deficiency is issued by the IRS Commissioner. Following this notice, taxpayers have 90 days to file a petition with the U.S. Tax Court to have their cases heard. If the 90 days pass without either the tax being paid or suit being filed, the IRS can assess a tax deficiency, enter judgment, and seize the taxpayer's property to collect the deficiency. However, no tax need be paid in advance for cases to be litigated in the Tax Court. Once a case has been docketed there, an appeals officer is assigned to the case and given exclusive authority to settle within a 4-month period. If no settlement is reached in that time, the case is scheduled for trial.

    Alternatively, the taxpayer may choose to pay the tax deficiency and then file a claim for a refund with the IRS. Unless a notice of claim disallowance is sent before 6 months expire, the taxpayer must wait that time period before he or she can file suit for a refund in either the U.S. District Court or the U.S. Court of Federal Claims.

14. The U.S. Tax Court was established for taxpayers who seek a redetermination of a deficiency asserted against them but do not wish first to pay the deficiency. Trial by jury is not available in the Tax Court. Questions of law and fact are decided by Tax Court judges.

    The U.S. District Court can only hear tax cases in which the taxpayer has first paid the deficiency and has been denied a refund by the IRS. The District Court is the only court in which a taxpayer may request a jury trial. In a case where there is a jury, the jury decides questions of fact; the judge decides questions of law.

    The U.S. Court of Federal Claims, like the U.S. District Court, can only hear tax cases in which the taxpayer has first paid the deficiency and has been denied a refund by the IRS. The Court of Federal Claims is a trial court that became operative on October 1, 1982, when the U.S. Court of Claims ceased to exist as such.

15. Answers:

    a. U.S. District Court
    b. Court of Appeals for the Federal Circuit
    c. U.S. Tax Court

16. The IRS does not consider itself bound by a Tax Court decision, a Court of Federal Claims decision, or a District Court decision (except for the particular case in which an adverse decision has been rendered). The U.S. Supreme Court is the highest court in the land and its decisions are required to be followed by the IRS as well as by taxpayers.

17. Appeals from the Tax Court by an unsuccessful taxpayer are heard by the U.S. Court of Appeals in the region of the country in which the taxpayer resides. If there is a difference of opinion in the various courts of appeal, the Tax Court follows the decisions of that Court of Appeals to which the taxpayer may appeal.

    Appeals from the Court of Federal Claims are heard by the Court of Appeals for the Federal Circuit, while appeals from a U.S. District Court are heard by that particular court's corresponding U.S. Court of Appeals. Appeals from a U.S. Court of Appeals or the Court of Appeals for the Federal Circuit are taken to the highest court in the land, the U.S. Supreme Court.

18. Supreme Court review of tax cases is generally available only if the Court itself grants petitions for appeal. Reasons for review typically are that (1) there is a conflict between

the courts of appeal for different circuits, or (2) an important and recurring problem in tax law administration is involved, or (3) many taxpayers are involved, or (4) the decision of a lower court conflicts with longstanding practice or existing legal authority.

19. Answers:

a.

(1) Joe will probably request an appeals conference. Assuming no agreement is reached, the IRS will send a statutory notice of deficiency for tax due. Joe now has 90 days to decide whether to pay or file suit. If he does not make a decision, the IRS may assess, obtain a judgment, and seize his property.

(2) Joe could file suit in the U.S. Tax Court. He pays no tax before the court (non-jury) decides the case. If Joe loses in the Tax Court, he can appeal to the court of appeals in his circuit (12 circuit courts), and finally, he can request the U.S. Supreme Court to hear the case. On the other hand, Joe could pay the tax due and sue for a refund in a U.S. district court. The district court judge decides the issue of law as to whether fines may be deductible as a business expense. If Joe loses on the legal issue, he may appeal to the Court of Appeals, and if he loses again, he may request the U.S. Supreme Court to hear the case. Appellate courts review only questions of law, not of fact. Or, Joe could pay the tax due and sue the government for a refund in the U.S. Court of Federal Claims. The Court of Federal Claims hears suits for tax refunds only. An adverse decision may be appealed to the Court of Appeals for the Federal Circuit and then on to the U.S. Supreme Court. Since the Supreme Court has discretion over cases it takes, it is unlikely the average case will be reviewed.

Joe will decide which court to sue in depending on the following considerations:

- precedent decisions of that particular court
- payment of tax before or after suit
- need for jury on sympathetic factual issue

b.

(1) The Internal Revenue Service is not bound by this decision in other similar cases even though Joe Smith is entitled to the deduction. The IRS may appeal a decision to the Third Circuit Court of Appeals. The IRS publishes lists of Tax Court cases to which it acquiesces or nonacquiesces.

(2) If Bill Zilch takes a deduction, the IRS will probably deny it. Bill must pay the tax or institute suit in one of three courts. Bill would probably choose the Tax Court because of the favorable precedent. The U.S. Supreme Court, as its name implies, is the final authority as to any question of federal law.

c.

(1) The Internal Revenue Service is not bound by this decision in other similar cases outside the Third Circuit, even though Joe's deduction was allowed in that circuit.

(2) The IRS will follow this decision in all Third Circuit cases. Roy Jones, who has the same truck route, could take the deductions knowing the IRS would not litigate.

(3) If Bill Zilch takes the deduction, the IRS will probably deny it. He must pay the tax or institute suit. If the IRS is upheld by the Ninth Circuit Court of Appeals (which covers Bill's area), then there is a conflict in the circuit courts. When this situation arises, it is more likely that the Supreme Court will grant a review.

d.  When the Supreme Court decides the case, all parties—Joe, Bill, Roy, and the IRS—are bound to follow the decision. The Supreme Court will hear appeals, in most cases, only where there is a conflict between decisions of lower courts, where the decision is probably in conflict with significant existing precedent, or where the issue is considered of major importance. The Supreme Court can choose (with few exceptions) which cases it will or will not hear. In other words, it can decline to hear the appeal by denying the petition for review. The U.S. Supreme Court, as its name implies, is the final authority as to any question of federal law.

# Self-Test Answers for Chapter 2

1. False. The original Constitution enacted in 1789 actually limited the original taxing power of the federal government by its uniformity and apportionment clauses under Article I, Sections 8 and 9. The 16th Amendment to the Constitution, passed in 1909, gave Congress the power to tax income from whatever source derived.

2. True.

3. True.

4. False. The bulk of the government's funds are produced through the federal income tax. Although the regulatory function is important, it is not more important than revenue production.

5. True.

6. False. The Internal Revenue Service is under the authority of the Department of the Treasury and the Secretary of the Treasury. The Secretary of the Treasury is responsible to the President of the United States. Therefore the source of authority for the Internal Revenue Service and the Treasury Department lies in the executive branch. The Internal Revenue Service is not responsible to Congress.

7. False. Each of the three coequal branches of the federal government—the legislative, the executive, and the judicial—has a major role in shaping the federal income tax system.

8. True.

9. True.

10. False. This statement applies to private rulings. Revenue rulings state the IRS's interpretation of an unclear point of law. They are usually based on a specific set of facts that involve a problem common to many taxpayers.

11. True.

12. False. The only trial court in which the taxpayer is entitled to a jury trial in a tax case is the U.S. District Court in the district in which the taxpayer resides. No jury trials are permitted either in the U.S. Tax Court or the U.S. Court of Federal Claims, which are the other two trial court tribunals.

13. False. Appeals from the U.S. Court of Federal Claims are heard by the Court of Appeals for the Federal Circuit, which is an Appellate Court. It is no longer possible to take appeals from a trial court directly to the U.S. Supreme Court.

14. False. The IRS does not consider itself bound beyond a particular case by court decisions other than those of the U.S. Supreme Court and those of a U.S. Circuit Court of Appeals with respect to cases arising in the same circuit.

15. True.

16. True.

17. False. A U.S. Court of Appeals for one circuit or region of the country need not follow the decisions of a U.S. Court of Appeals for another circuit.

18. False. In general, review of cases by the Supreme Court is subject to the discretion of the Supreme Court itself.

19. False. Decisions of the Supreme Court are binding on all lower courts and administrative agencies, including the IRS.

# Chapter 3

## Answers to Review Questions

1.  The Internal Revenue Code defines gross income as "all income from whatever source derived," including (but not limited to) the following 15 items:

    *   compensation for services, including fees, commissions, fringe benefits, and similar items
    *   gross income derived from business
    *   gains derived from dealings in property
    *   interest
    *   rents
    *   royalties
    *   dividends
    *   alimony and separate maintenance payments
    *   annuities
    *   income from life insurance and endowment contracts
    *   pensions
    *   income from discharge of indebtedness
    *   distributive share of partnership gross income
    *   income in respect of a decedent
    *   income from an interest in an estate or trust

2.  Income is subject to income taxation, while capital is not. Therefore, the receipt of an item of income (in whatever form) is an event subject to income taxation, while the receipt, return, or replacement of a capital item is not a taxable event.

3.  Don has not realized income because there has been no disposition of the property.

4.  Mrs. Eidson has received income when interest earned on her life insurance policy dividends is credited to her policy account. Even though she has not actually reduced the income to her possession, she has received it constructively. The income tax regulations state that income must be included in a taxpayer's gross income for the taxable year in which it is "actually or constructively received." The regulations elaborate by stating that even though income is not actually reduced to a taxpayer's possession, the taxpayer is deemed to have constructively received it in the taxable year during which (1) it is credited to the taxpayer's account, as in the case of Mrs. Eidson, (2) set apart for the taxpayer, or (3) otherwise made available to be drawn from at any time.

5.  Courts have held that Sec. 61 of the Code is broad enough to include as taxable income any economic or financial benefit conferred on an employee as compensation, regardless of its form. This concept is known as the economic-benefit theory or doctrine, and it has been applied to situations involving a payment in kind or where the employer has made available to the employee the equivalent of cash—in other words, when the employee receives from the employer something with a current, real, and measurable value.

6.  Paul receives an economic benefit from his employer intended as compensation in the form of life insurance premium payments. Therefore the amount of the premium is ordinary income to Paul.

7.  The principle of assignment of income provides that the taxation of income cannot be shifted from one taxpayer to another merely by transferring or assigning to another taxpayer the right to receive the income. Consequently, the taxpayer whose personal efforts generated the income or who is the owner of the property that generated the income must report or declare the income on his or her own tax return. Assigning the

income to another taxpayer (such as a family member whose marginal rate of taxation is lower) will not shift the burden of taxation for the income to that taxpayer.

8.  Jones, not his daughter, would be taxed on commissions based on the assignment-of-income doctrine. Jones cannot assign income that he has earned to another party.

# Self-Test Answers for Chapter 3

1. True.
2. True.
3. False. A return of capital is not "income" for tax purposes.
4. True.
5. True.
6. False. The doctrine of constructive receipt is used in determining when an item is included in income, not in determining which item is income.
7. False. The economic-benefit theory taxes as income any economic or financial benefit conferred on the employee regardless of its form, as long as the employee receives something with a current, real, and measurable value. Use of a car for personal purposes constitutes such an economic benefit.
8. False. Income is always taxed to the person who earns it, creates the right to receive it, or enjoys its benefit, or to the person who earns or controls the property that is the source of the income. Therefore, while it is possible to assign income that one has earned to another person, it will still be taxed to the person who earned the income.

# Chapter 4

## Answers to Review Questions

1. Answers:

   a. The calculation of an individual taxpayer's adjusted gross income (AGI) is an intermediate step in the process of determining taxable income. To ascertain AGI, certain deductions are subtracted from the taxpayer's gross income. These deductions are referred to as "above-the-line" deductions and are available regardless of whether the taxpayer claims "itemized" deductions. Above-the-line deductions reduce AGI, which is one of the most important tax planning objectives for individual taxpayers because if AGI exceeds certain specified amounts, many tax benefits are either reduced or "phased out."

   b. Above-the-line deductions generally relate to business or income-producing activities of the taxpayer. Although not an all-inclusive list, the following are several of the more important above-the-line deductions claimed by individual taxpayers:

      - deductible contributions to pension and profit-sharing plans of self-employed individuals
      - deductible alimony payments
      - deductible moving expenses
      - contributions to medical savings accounts or health savings accounts
      - deductible contributions to IRAs
      - deductible interest payments made on qualified education loans
      - penalties or other forfeitures resulting from premature withdrawals from time savings accounts or deposits

      The textbook also lists additional items.

2. The standard deduction is a specified amount, indexed annually for inflation, that may be claimed in calculating taxable income by taxpayers who do not itemize their deductions. The amount of the taxpayer's standard deduction is based on filing status. Increased amounts are available for blind taxpayers and taxpayers aged 65 and over. In choosing between itemizing deductions and taking the standard deduction, the typical taxpayer would opt to itemize if the total amount of such deductions exceeds the applicable standard deduction.

3. Dependents are not eligible to claim the regular standard deduction amounts on their own tax returns. The special standard deduction amount allowable on a dependent's tax return is the greater of a specified dollar amount, or a smaller dollar amount plus the dependent's earned income for the year (but not more than the regular standard deduction amount). The dollar amounts are indexed annually for inflation.

4. A special rule applies to taxpayers who are 65 years of age or older and/or are legally blind. Such taxpayers (including dependents) are entitled to increase their standard deduction by specified amounts. For married taxpayers filing jointly, each spouse who qualifies may add the additional amount or amounts to the standard deduction claimed on the joint return.

5. Answers:

   a. If an individual taxpayer's AGI exceeds a specified threshold amount (that is indexed annually for inflation), his or her itemized deductions are reduced by 3 percent of the amount by which AGI exceeds the threshold amount. If itemized deductions are reduced by the overall limitation, the reduction cannot exceed 80 percent of the total itemized deductions that are subject to the reduction.

b. The overall limitation on itemized deductions does not apply to deductions for medical expenses, investment interest expenses, casualty and theft losses, or allowable gambling losses. Moreover, the overall limitation on itemized deductions is applied only after the rules and limits for each specific itemized deduction have been applied. These specific rules include the 50 percent of AGI "ceiling" on charitable contributions, the dollar amount loan limits for qualified residence interest, and the 2 percent of AGI "floor" on most miscellaneous itemized deductions.

6. Answers:
    a. The personal exemption amount is indexed annually for inflation by applying an indexing factor to each year's exemption amount.
    b. A taxpayer who may be claimed as a dependent of another taxpayer is not entitled to a personal exemption for himself or herself.

7. Answers:
    a. A taxpayer is entitled to claim one additional exemption for each individual who is a dependent of the taxpayer. This dependency exemption is allowable regardless of whether the taxpayer claims the standard deduction or itemizes deductions. Each exemption is the equivalent of a deduction from AGI for a specified amount (that is indexed annually for inflation). The amount is the same as the personal exemption amount.
    b. A taxpayer may claim any individual as a dependent who meets the definition of either a "qualifying child" or a "qualifying relative." Such individuals must also meet the following additional requirements:
        • First, the individual being claimed as a dependent may not claim any other individual as his or her own dependent for income tax purposes.
        • Second, the individual being claimed as a dependent may generally not file a joint return with his or her spouse for the year.
        • Third, an individual who is not a U.S. citizen or national generally cannot be claimed as a dependent unless that individual is a resident of either the United States or a country contiguous to the United States. However, a legally adopted child of the taxpayer (or one legally placed for adoption) can be claimed as a dependent of the taxpayer if the child has the same principal place of abode as the taxpayer for the year and is a member of the taxpayer's household (provided that the taxpayer is a U.S. citizen or national).

8. First, if only one of the taxpayers eligible to claim an individual is a parent of that individual, the parent is entitled to the exemption. This can occur, for example, where both a grandparent and a parent are eligible. Second, if a child's parents don't file a joint return, and each of them is eligible to claim the child as a dependent, the parent with whom the child resided for the longer period of time during the year gets the exemption. If that amount of time is equal, then the parent with the greater amount of adjusted gross income (AGI) for the year gets the exemption. Third, if the child or other individual is not claimed as a dependent by either of his or her parents, and other taxpayers are able to claim the individual as a dependent, then the taxpayer with the highest AGI for the year gets the exemption. Note that these rules will apply where more than one taxpayer attempts to claim an exemption for the same person.

9. Each personal and dependency exemption otherwise allowable to a taxpayer is phased out by 2 percent of each $2,500 or any fraction of $2,500 by which AGI is in excess of the threshold amount (the amount is $1,250 for married taxpayers filing separately). The

threshold income levels for the phaseout are based on AGI, are indexed annually for inflation, and vary according to the filing status of the taxpayer.

10. In addition to the marginal rate of tax imposed by the Code, taxpayers lose deductions (and/or credits) with each additional increment of income that results in phaseouts. Therefore the actual effective tax rate on the increments of income that result in the phaseout of tax benefits may be significantly higher than the statutory marginal rate.

11. The general rule for claiming a dependency exemption for a child of divorced or separated parents is that the custodial parent is entitled to the dependency exemption. However, if the custodial parent signs a written declaration that he or she will not claim the child as a dependent for tax purposes (that is, "releases" the exemption), the noncustodial parent may claim the exemption if the written declaration is attached to his or her tax return. A "custodial parent" for this purpose is the parent who has custody of the child for the greater portion of the calendar year. This rule applies regardless of the general requirement that a "qualifying child" have the same principal place of abode as the taxpayer.

12. There are six basic federal income tax rates under current law. The lowest marginal tax rates are 10 and 15 percent. The highest marginal rate is currently 35 percent.

13. The filing status for taxpayers other than corporations includes the following five groups:

    - married taxpayers filing jointly
    - unmarried heads of households
    - unmarried or single taxpayers
    - married taxpayers filing separately
    - estates and trusts

14. The general rule is that each spouse is jointly and severally liable for the tax payable with respect to a joint return. However, the "innocent spouse" rules may provide an exception to this treatment for a spouse who qualifies under those rules.

15. Answers:

    a. A "surviving spouse" is permitted to file and use the tax brackets applicable to joint returns. To qualify for joint return status, the surviving spouse must maintain a household that includes a son, stepson, daughter, or stepdaughter who is eligible to be claimed as a dependent under the dependency exemption rules. The surviving spouse must furnish over half the cost of maintaining the household.
    b. The surviving spouse may file under the joint return status for a period of 2 years, beginning with the year following the year of the spouse's death.

16. The rules for qualifying as an unmarried head of household can be briefly summarized as follows:

    - the marital status requirement. The taxpayer must be unmarried at the close of the taxable year except when he or she is considered an abandoned spouse.
    - the household requirement. The taxpayer must maintain a household and furnish over half the cost of doing so during the taxable year.
    - the qualifying person requirement. A qualifying person must generally be a member of the taxpayer's household for more than one-half of the taxable year. That person must be either a "qualifying child" of the taxpayer under the dependency exemption rules, or a "qualifying relative" under those rules who is actually related to the taxpayer.
    - the rule for parents. A parent may be a qualifying person, even if the parent does not live in the taxpayer's household but can still be claimed by the taxpayer as a dependent while living in a long-term care facility.

17. Since parents generally have more income than their young children, they desire to transfer investment assets to the children to gain the benefit of lower marginal tax rates. The "kiddie tax" is designed to prevent the parents from shifting large amounts of unearned income to their children and making the shift effective for income tax purposes.

18. The mechanics of the kiddie tax can be summarized as follows:

    - If a child under a specified age has unearned income above a specified amount, the excess is taxed at the highest marginal rate applicable to the child's parents for the year rather than at the child's marginal rate.
    - It applies to unearned income generated by any asset the child owns, regardless of when or by whom the asset was transferred to the child (except for income from certain qualified disability trusts).
    - The additional tax paid with the child's return is equal to the difference between the tax payable at the child's rates and the amount of tax the parents would have paid on the net unearned income if it had been included on the parent's return.
    - It applies only if a child has at least one parent living at the end of the taxable year.
    - It does not apply if the child is married and files a joint return with his or her spouse.
    - The rules become more complicated if a child has both earned and unearned income.

19. Yes, the kiddie tax rules call for net unearned income of children under a specified age to be taxed at the marginal rate of the parents, not just unearned income generated by assets received from the child's parents. Therefore, income generated by assets gifted by grandparents is generally subject to the kiddie tax.

20. Individuals are generally required to file income tax returns by April 15, unless an extension is obtained.

# Self-Test Answers for Chapter 4

1. True.
2. False. The standard deduction amount varies according to the taxpayer's filing status. These amounts are indexed annually for inflation.
3. True.
4. False. If a taxpayer can be claimed as a dependent of another taxpayer, that person is not entitled to a personal exemption for himself or herself.
5. True.
6. False. A taxpayer may generally not claim a personal exemption for a child who is married and files a joint return with his or her spouse.
7. True.
8. True.
9. False. The lowest marginal rate is currently 10 percent.
10. True.
11. True.
12. True.
13. False. The kiddie tax rules generally apply to unearned income of a child, regardless of whether the income-producing assets were received from the child's parents.
14. False. Corporations are required to file returns by the 15th day of the third month following the close of the taxable year.

# Chapter 5

## Answers to Review Questions

1. The basic rule for alimony or separate maintenance payments is that they are includible in the gross income of the payee. Correspondingly, alimony payments includible in the gross income of the payee are deductible for income tax purposes from the gross income of the payer.

2. Alimony payments are required to be in cash or a cash equivalent. Because of this requirement, such benefits as the rent-free occupancy of a home by a former spouse and the couple's children cannot be treated as alimony payments for tax purposes.

3. Answers:

    a. The payer of an "excess alimony payment" is required to include the excess payment in his or her gross income in the third postseparation year.

    b. The calculation of an "excess" alimony payment is based on the relative amounts of the payments made during the first 3 postseparation years. In computing the "excess" alimony payment, compare the second postseparation year to the third postseparation year payment. The second year's "excess" payment is the amount by which the second year payment exceeds the payment in the third postseparation year plus $15,000. In the payer's first postseparation tax year, the "excess" payment is computed by taking the average of the alimony payments in the second and third postseparation years as adjusted by the initial calculation and adding $15,000 to that figure. Any alimony payment for the first postseparation year that is in excess of that amount is the "excess" alimony payment for the first year payment. The total "excess" alimony payment that needs to be recaptured is the combination of both calculations.

       If either spouse dies before the end of the third postseparation year, or if either spouse remarries before the end of that year and payments cease as a result of such event, then the front-loading rules for excess alimony payments do not apply.

4. Payments for support of minor children are not treated as alimony for tax purposes. Such payments are not deductible by the payer spouse and not includible in the gross income of the payee spouse. Payments are treated as child support to the extent that the terms of the applicable divorce or separation agreement fix or designate them as such. For purposes of this rule, a provision in the agreement calling for a reduction in payments based on certain specified contingencies relating to a child is considered to be designating such payments as child support. These contingencies include a reduction in payments happening at the time or associated with the time when a child attains a specified age, marries, leaves school, or dies. The amount of the reduction in the payment that would result from the occurrence of one of these contingencies under the agreement is the amount treated as child support for tax purposes.

5. Perhaps the most common arrangement is to transfer the ownership of an existing life policy that insures the life of one spouse to the other spouse. The transfer of the policy itself does not have income tax consequences for either spouse regardless of the policy's cash value. Such a transfer is neither alimony nor child support, but a nontaxable transfer of property incident to a divorce. However, if the spouse who transferred the policy is obligated to continue to pay premiums on the transferred policy, the payment of such premiums is generally treated as an alimony payment.

    The transfer of a life insurance policy will not cause the subsequent payment of death benefits to be subject to income tax under the "transfer-for-value" rule. Transfers incident to divorce are not subject to the transfer-for-value rule. Therefore such death benefits retain their income-tax-free character.

6. Answers:

   a. Each $150 payment is income to Helen and a deduction for Bob because the payments are pursuant to a divorce decree and no part of the payments is an excess alimony payment. Also, there is no requirement that the decree must specifically state that payments will cease at Helen's death in order to claim a deduction. There is no deduction for child support payments, so the $100 child support for Timmy will neither be deductible by Bob nor includible in Helen's income.

   b. Although Helen possibly has an economic benefit here, the Internal Revenue Service does not consider rent-free occupancy to be taxable alimony.

   c.

      (1) Helen, as absolute owner of the transferred life insurance policy, has income upon payment of the whole life policy premium. Likewise, Bob may deduct his whole life premium. The payment of premiums for the new whole life policy does not give rise to either income or a deduction, since Helen is not the absolute owner of the policy.

      (2) Such life insurance proceeds will be exempt from income tax.

7. Answers:

   a. The general theory of annuity taxation involves the concept that the contract owner's capital investment in the contract may be recovered tax free when distributions are made. However, the interest or other earnings on the contract funds must be subject to taxation at some point in time.

   b. The income taxation of a payment in the form of a full or immediate payment annuity is determined by using a fraction called the "exclusion ratio." The numerator of the fraction is the amount of the "investment in the contract." The denominator of the fraction is the total "expected return" under the contract. The periodic annuity payment is multiplied by this fraction to calculate the portion of the payment that is received tax free by the annuitant as a return of the investment in the contract. The balance of the payment is taxable to the annuitant.

      The "investment in the contract" may be defined as the aggregate amount of premiums or other consideration paid for the contract minus any distributions already made from the contract that were excludible from the recipient's gross income as a return of capital.

      The "expected return" under the contract may be defined as the total of the amounts that are expected to be received in the form of an annuity under the contract. If the annuity payment is calculated using the life expectancy of one or more annuitants, the expected return is calculated by reference to actuarial tables found in the Treasury regulations promulgated pursuant to IRC Sec. 72.

      An exclusion ratio can be calculated for a partial annuitization meeting the requirements of section 72 (a) (2) under similar principles. If any amount is received as an annuity for at least 10 years or during the lives of one or more individuals, then that portion of the annuity contract is treated as a separate contract for calculation of the exclusion ratio. The investment in the contract is allocated pro rata between each portion of the annuity contract from which amounts (a) are received as annuity and (b) the portion of the contract from which amounts are *not* received as an annuity.

8. Answers:
     a. $13,000
     b. $100 × 12 × 13.2 = $15,840
     c. $13,000 ÷ $15,840 = .8207 × $1,200 = $984.84
     d. $1,200 − $984.84 = $215.16

9. The refund feature would be subtracted from the investment in the contract before the exclusion ratio is determined. Therefore the investment in the contract would be $11,000 ($13,000 − $2,000), and the exclusion ratio would be .694 ($11,000 ÷ $15,840). The amount excluded from income annually is $832.80 (.694 × $1,200). Taxable income is $367.20 ($1,200 − $832.80).

10. Answers:
     a. If the annuitant lives beyond his or her period of life expectancy as determined under the regulations, no exclusion ratio is applied to payments received after the end of the life expectancy period. Therefore the full amount of payments received after the life expectancy period will be taxable.
     b. Yes, the tax treatment is different for individuals whose annuity starting dates commenced before January 1, 1987. If the annuitant under such contracts lives beyond his or her life expectancy, the exclusion ratio is applied to payments for as long as the annuitant lives, making it possible for the annuitant to recover a total amount tax free that is more than the actual investment in the contract.

11. Answers:
     a. An annuity that provides for income payments to be made as long as either of two persons live is known as a joint and survivor annuity. In its most common form, it continues the same fixed amount of income to the survivor as is payable while both annuitants are alive. A common modification provides that the income to the survivor will be reduced to either two-thirds or one-half of the original amount. In other words, a joint and survivor annuity provides for the payment of a fixed amount of income while two annuitants live, then upon the death of one, it continues to pay the same or a lesser amount of income to the survivor for the duration of his or her life.
     b. The expected return under a joint and survivor annuity can be calculated by using the tables contained in the Treasury regulations pursuant to Code Sec. 72. These tables provide the joint life expectancy for two annuitants depending on their individual ages.

12. Answers:
     a. $22,000
     b. $27,600 ($1,200 × 23 years = $27,600)
     c. $956.52
     d. $243.48

13. In the case of a variable annuity, the "expected return" under the contract cannot be accurately calculated for purposes of determining an exclusion ratio for the annuity payments. Therefore the exclusion ratio calculation is not used to determine the taxation of the annuity payments under a variable contract. Consequently, the investment in a variable contract is divided by the number of years of the annuitant's life expectancy to determine the dollar amount of each payment that is excludible from the annuitant's gross income.

14. Because the variable annuity payments are subject to fluctuations, it is possible that the amount of an annuity payment under a variable contract will be less than the amount of

each payment that was determined to be excludible. In such cases, the entire payment will be excludible from gross income, and the "unused" portion of the excludible amount can be recovered later for income tax purposes by recomputing the annual dollar amount of the annuity payment that is excludible from gross income. The recomputation of the excludible amount can be made at the election of the annuitant and is accomplished by the following steps:

- The dollar amount of the exclusion that was not utilized is determined.
- The annuitant's life expectancy at the time of the recomputation is found by consulting the appropriate table in the regulations.
- An additional excludible amount is determined by dividing the amount of the unused exclusion by the life expectancy of the annuitant at the time of the election to recompute.
- The additional amount is then added to the original excludible amount to determine the adjusted excludible amount.

15. Answers:

   a. $25,000
   b. $25,000 ÷ 14.4 years = $1,736.11
   c. Mr. Glikes has a $236.11 unused exclusion that he may add proportionately over his remaining life expectancy to the original amount excludible annually. His new excludible amount is $1,762.06 ([$236.11 ÷ 9.1 years] + $1,736.11).

16. A partial withdrawal of funds from a deferred annuity contract is treated as a taxable event for income tax purposes. The general rule is that the withdrawn amount will be taxed to the extent of "income on the contract." "Income on the contract" is the amount by which the cash value of the contract (without regard to surrender charges) exceeds the owner's investment in the contract. This is a form of "LIFO" (last-in, first-out) taxation in which the earnings on the contract are taxed before the investment in the contract can be recovered tax free as a return of capital.

    This "LIFO" rule of income taxation applies to annuity contracts that were funded after August 13, 1982. Contracts funded on or before this date follow a FIFO rule of taxation for withdrawals.

17. There is a 10 percent penalty tax that generally applies to amounts received from annuity contracts that

- are not received in the form of annuity payments and
- are received by a taxpayer who has not attained the age of 59 1/2

    It applies only to the portion of any withdrawal, loan, or collateralization of the contract that is taxable under the rules pertaining to "amounts not received as an annuity." Moreover, the penalty is in addition to the regular income tax, but it does not apply to any portion of the transaction that is treated as a nontaxable return of capital.

18. To qualify as group term insurance under Sec. 79, the insurance must meet the following conditions:

   a. It must provide a death benefit excludible from federal income tax.
   b. It must be provided to a group of employees.
   c. It must be provided under a policy carried directly or indirectly by the employer.
   d. The plan must be arranged in such a manner as to preclude individual selection of coverage amounts.

19. Under Sec. 79 the cost of the first $50,000 of coverage is not taxed to the employee. The cost of coverage in excess of $50,000, less any employee contributions for the entire amount of coverage, represents taxable income to the employee. For purposes of Sec. 79, the cost of this excess coverage is determined by a government table called the Uniform Premium Table I.

20. Answers:

a. The amount of taxable income is determined by using the Uniform Premium Table I cost for the amount of coverage in excess of $50,000.

| | |
|---|---|
| Coverage provided: | $75,000 |
| Less Sec. 79 exclusion: | $50,000 |
| Amount subject to taxation: | $25,000 |
| Uniform Premium Table I monthly cost per $1,000 of coverage at age 32: | $ 0.08 |
| Monthly cost ($0.08 x 25): | $ 2.00 |
| Annual cost ($2 x 12): | $24.00 of taxable income |

b. The full $36 annual contribution could have been deducted from the Table I annual cost of $24. Therefore no income would have resulted from the group insurance coverage.

21. Any plan that qualifies as group term insurance under Sec. 79 is subject to nondiscrimination rules, and the $50,000 exclusion will not be available to key employees if a plan is discriminatory. Such a plan might favor key employees in either eligibility or benefits. If the plan is discriminatory, the value of the full amount of coverage for key employees, minus their own contributions, will be considered taxable income, based on the greater of actual or Table I costs.

22. Generally, death proceeds under a group term insurance contract do not result in taxable income to the beneficiary if paid in a lump sum.

23. The courts have held that an employee who receives property as payment for the performance of services must include its value in income in the year in which he or she becomes vested in the value of the property. The court-made rules in this area are sometimes summarized as the "economic benefit doctrine." This doctrine as it applies to property transferred for services is codified in Code Sec. 83, which provides that the value of property that is transferred for services is included in income "at the first time the rights of the person having the beneficial interest in such property are transferable or are not subject to a substantial risk of forfeiture."

24. Sec. 83(c)(1) provides that "the rights of a person in property are subject to a substantial risk of forfeiture if such person's rights to full enjoyment of such property are conditioned upon the future performance of substantial services by any individual."

The Committee Reports for Sec. 83 state that "In other cases (besides those involving service conditions) the question of whether there is a substantial risk of forfeiture depends upon the facts and circumstances." For example, the regulations state that where an employee receives property from an employer subject to a requirement that it be returned if the total earnings of the employer do not increase, such property is subject to a substantial risk of forfeiture. Note that this performance standard does not actually involve a requirement that services be performed. Moreover, the regulations also state that a forfeiture provision can be valid if it is related to the purpose of the transfer. A performance standard is an example of this type of provision.

25. If an employee receives restricted property and wants to include it in income currently, he or she can elect under Sec. 83(b) to include the current (fair market) value in income currently. The current value of the property is determined without regard to restrictions (except for one that will not lapse).

26. Under Sec. 83(h) the employer's deduction is equal to the amount included in income by the employee and is deducted in the year in which the employee includes the amount.

# Self-Test Answers for Chapter 5

1. True.
2. False. Alimony payments must be made in cash.
3. True.
4. True.
5. False. Although a divorce decree sometimes allows the custodial spouse and children rent-free occupancy of the family home, the value of a similar rental is not treated as alimony.
6. False. Child support does not constitute alimony for tax purposes and is not deductible to the payer-spouse.
7. False. When a former husband retains a life insurance policy and merely names his wife revocable beneficiary, he has retained all economic rights and benefits of the policy. Therefore, although he pays the premiums, the premium payments are neither deductible by him nor taxable to the wife as alimony.
8. True.
9. True.
10. True.
11. False. A refund feature provides that, if the annuitant dies before receiving a stated number of payments or a specified amount of payments, remaining payments will be made to a specified beneficiary.
12. True.
13. False. A withdrawal of investment amounts from deferred-annuity contracts prior to the annuity starting date will generally cause immediate income taxation to the extent the cash surrender value exceeds the investment in the contract. (Different rules apply to annuities funded before August 14, 1982.) There is also a 10 percent penalty tax on any taxable amount withdrawn prior to the annuity starting date if the taxpayer has not reached age 59½, subject to certain exceptions.
14. False. Employer contributions for employee group term coverage are generally deductible by the employer.
15. False. An insured employee may exclude the value of premiums representing the first $50,000 of coverage if certain nondiscrimination rules are met.
16. True.
17. False. A group plan that covers fewer than 10 employees may provide either a flat amount of coverage, a uniform percentage of salary, or an amount based on certain employee classifications.
18. False. Restricted stock is stock that is given or sold at a reduced price to an employee and is subject to provisions which involve a substantial risk of forfeiture.
19. True.
20. True.
21. True.

# Chapter 6

## Answers to Review Questions

1. The value of money or property received as a gift, bequest, devise, or inheritance is generally excluded from gross income under Code Sec. 102.

2. A gift is defined as a gratuitous transfer of property. To be considered a gift, the following elements are essential:

   - a donor competent to make the gift
   - a clear and unmistakable intention on the donor's behalf to make the gift
   - a donee capable of receiving the gift
   - an irrevocable conveyance, assignment, or transfer sufficient to vest legal title to the property in the donee
   - a donor's relinquishment of dominion and control of the property by delivery to the donee.

     In order to have a valid gift for federal income tax purposes, the donor must have acted out of a "detached and disinterested" generosity in transferring the property. Gifts are normally made out of "affection, respect, admiration, charity, or like impulses." Valid gifts have no strings attached.

3. Questions regarding gift or compensation normally arise as to payments where there is a past or present employment relationship. For federal income tax law purposes, a voluntary transfer without compensation is not necessarily a gift. It is not a gift if there is a legal or moral obligation for the transfer or if the donor expects to receive a benefit from the "gift." However, the mere absence of a legal or moral obligation for the transfer does not necessarily qualify the transfer as a gift. A transfer is a gift if it is made from detached or disinterested generosity. Ultimately, the question of gift or compensation is resolved by reviewing the donor's dominant reason for making the transfer. Amounts transferred from an employer to an employee will not generally be treated as gifts.

4. Answers:

   a. The general rule is that gross income does not include the value of property acquired by gift.
   b. Rental income from the property will be taxed to Scoop.
   c. If James gives Scoop the right to income only, the income will be taxed to James under the assignment-of-income doctrine discussed in chapter 3.

5. A bequest of a specific sum of money or property is generally excluded from income for tax purposes even when it is paid out of income. This treatment applies only if the bequest is paid or credited all at once or in not more than three installments. If the bequest is paid in more than three installments, it is taxable to the recipient to the extent it is actually paid from the income generated.

6. Answers:

   a. The specific bequest of $80,000 to Mrs. Blair will be excluded from income taxation even though the executor pays the bequest out of the estate's income. This exemption will apply provided the bequest is paid to Mrs. Blair in no more than three installments. Therefore, if payment is made in two annual installments, the $80,000 bequest will be exempt from income taxation.
   b. If the will directs that the specific bequest of $80,000 is to be paid in equal annual amounts over 5 years, Mrs. Blair must pay income tax annually on each $16,000 installment to the extent it is paid out of the estate's income.

7. Sec. 103 of the Code provides that interest earned on certain obligations of a state are tax exempt and therefore excluded from gross income. In addition, interest earned on the obligations of a political subdivision of a state (that is, a county, city, and/or town) is also exempt from federal income taxation. Such tax-exempt state and municipal bonds are generally public purpose bonds; that is, bonds used to finance essential governmental activities.

8. The equivalent yield is 9.23 percent at Frank's marginal tax rate of 35 percent, and is derived as follows: 6% ÷ .65 (1.00 − .35 marginal tax bracket).

9. Answers:

   a. State and municipal "public purpose" bonds are tax-exempt with respect to interest earned. This means that 100 percent of the interest income received by an investor is generally free from federal taxation.

   b. The interest income from "nongovernmental purpose" bonds is not subject to the regular federal income tax. However, the income from these bonds is subject to the alternative minimum tax.

   c. The interest income of arbitrage bonds, industrial development bonds, and most other private activity bonds is subject to the regular federal income tax. Obligations issued under this category may include sports facilities, convention or trade show facilities, parking facilities, and air and water pollution control facilities. These bonds are considered taxable municipal bonds.

   d. Municipal bonds issued before August 7, 1986, generate tax-exempt interest to the extent they were exempt under prior law.

10. Answers:

   a. Obligations issued to finance the construction of a waste disposal facility are considered to be tax-free public purpose municipal bonds.

   b. Obligations issued to finance the construction of a convention facility are considered to be taxable municipal bonds, which are subject to the regular federal income tax.

   c. Obligations issued to finance subsidized housing are considered to be "nongovernmental purpose" bonds, which are not subject to the regular federal income tax but are subject to the alternative minimum tax.

11. No, interest income earned on U.S. savings bonds is taxable. Taxpayers have a choice of including the incremental interest income annually or reporting the entire amount of interest income over the life of the bond upon redemption.

12. If a tax-exempt security is sold at a gain, the gain is taxable in computing gross income.

13. The Stevens's provisional income is $28,500 ($3,000 tax-exempt interest plus $5,000 taxable interest plus $12,000 pension income plus one-half of their Social Security benefits of $17,000). This amount is less than the applicable first-tier base amount of $32,000. Therefore, their benefits are fully excludible from gross income.

14. Medical expense reimbursements from accident and health insurance plans are excluded from gross income to the extent the taxpayer has not claimed a medical expense deduction for the underlying medical costs as an itemized deduction.

15. Code Sec. 104 prohibits the exclusion of punitive damages. Therefore, punitive damages paid pursuant to an action for personal injury are fully taxable for federal income tax purposes.

16. Financial awards related to emotional distress are generally not excludible from gross income under current law. There would be an exclusion from gross income if the

emotional distress award was attributed to a physical injury or sickness or represents reimbursement for medical expenses arising from the emotional distress.

17. Answers:

   a. The general rule is to tax amounts received for personal injuries or sickness under accident and health plans to employees where the employer pays for the cost of the plan.

   b. An exception to the general rule excludes from gross income amounts received as reimbursements from an accident or health plan for the medical care of the taxpayer, his or her spouse, or dependents. These benefits are excludible if an insurance company provides the accident and health insurance benefits.

   c. An exception to the general rule excludes payments unrelated to absence from work. If the taxpayer, his or her spouse, or a dependent incurs an injury that results in permanent disfigurement, loss or loss of using a body part, or loss of a bodily function, then the amounts received under the employer's accident or health care plan are excluded from gross income. However, no exclusion is permitted if the length of time an employee is absent from work is a factor in determining the amount of the payment (that is, disability income proceeds).

18. Qualified long-term care insurance is treated as accident or health insurance under Code Secs. 104 through 106. As a medical expense reimbursement, long-term care reimbursements up to a specified amount per day (as adjusted for inflation) per covered individual are excluded from gross income. Amounts in excess of the daily exclusion are also excluded from gross income to the extent that actual long-term care expenses exceed the daily benefit and are not otherwise reimbursed. In an employer-provided long-term care insurance plan, amounts received are treated in generally the same way as amounts received for medical care.

19. Answers:

   a. An employee's gross income does not include premiums paid by an employer for accident or health care insurance coverage for the employee, the employee's spouse, and the employee's dependents.

   b. In general, the employer may claim a tax deduction for premiums paid for accident and health care coverage for employees.

20. Answers:

   a. A self-funded medical reimbursement plan is one under which the employer will either pay the providers of medical care directly or reimburse employees for their medical expenses. If the plan meets certain nondiscrimination requirements, employees will have no taxable income. If the plan is discriminatory, all or a portion of the benefits received by "highly compensated individuals" will be treated as taxable income. Whether the plan is discriminatory or not, the employer will receive an income tax deduction for benefit payments as they are made.

   b. To be considered nondiscriminatory, a self-funded plan must meet certain requirements regarding eligibility and benefits. For eligibility purposes, the plan must provide benefits for 70 percent or more of all employees or for 80 percent or more of all eligible employees if 70 percent or more of all employees are eligible. Certain employees can be excluded from the all-employees category, including employees who have not completed 3 years of service, employees who have not attained age 25, part-time employees, seasonal employees, and employees who are covered by a collective-bargaining agreement if accident and health benefits were a subject of collective bargaining.

If the plan fails to meet the percentage test regarding eligibility, it can still qualify as nondiscriminatory if the IRS is satisfied that it does not discriminate. To satisfy the nondiscrimination requirements for benefits, the same type and amount of benefits must be provided for all employees under the plan regardless of their compensation. In addition, the dependents of other employees cannot be treated less favorably than the dependents of highly compensated individuals.

c.  If highly compensated individuals covered under a self-funded plan receive any benefits not available to all employees in the plan, these benefits are considered an excess reimbursement and must be included in their gross income for income tax purposes. If the plan discriminates in the way it determines eligibility, then highly compensated individuals will have excess reimbursements for any amounts they receive. The amount of this excess reimbursement is determined by a percentage that is calculated by dividing the total amount of benefits received by highly compensated individuals (exclusive of any other excess reimbursements) by the total amount of benefits paid to all employees. It is possible that a plan might discriminate with respect to both eligibility and benefits.

21. Answers:

a.  If the secretary's actual medical expenses amounted to $1,000 but were not limited to that figure, then there would not be discrimination. However, if certain limitations were placed on her reimbursable amounts and not on the highly compensated employee, then there would be discrimination in benefits.

b.  Assume that there is discrimination and the secretary's reimbursement is typical of other nonhighly compensated employees in that they received 25 percent of the highly compensated employee's benefit ($4,000 versus $1,000). The highly compensated employee would have received an excess reimbursement of $3,000 ($4,000 - $1,000) that would be includible in his gross income for this year.

22. Bob and Frieda may exclude $5,000 of the $7,000 benefit they receive, the maximum amount excludible. Therefore the remaining $2,000 will be taxed to Bob and Frieda.

# Self-Test Answers for Chapter 6

1. True.
2. True.
3. False. Income received from a gift is not subject to exclusion as a gift. If the income is otherwise taxable, it must be included in the donee's gross income.
4. True.
5. True.
6. True.
7. True.
8. False. Interest earned on United States obligations is generally fully taxable as ordinary income unless the bond qualifies for the exclusion for Series EE bonds used to pay educational expenses.
9. False. A tax-exempt municipal obligation means that the interest received may be excluded from gross income. If a gain is made on the sale of the municipal obligation, then the gain realized is currently taxable.
10. True.
11. False. This base amount is $32,000.
12. True.
13. True.
14. True.
15. False. Damages that are paid for lost wages are not excludible from gross income. Rather, damages paid for physical injuries are excludible under IRC Sec. 104, subject to special rules for punitive damages and damages for emotional distress.
16. False. Employer-financed medical expense benefits are generally tax exempt if they provide reimbursement for the medical expenses of an employee or the employee's spouse or dependents.
17. True.
18. True.
19. False. Employer contributions to an accident and health plan are not included in the gross income of employees.
20. True.
21. False. A single parent can exclude up to $5,000 of benefits under a qualified dependent-care assistance program.

# Chapter 7

## Answers to Review Questions

1. Code Sec. 162 states that there shall be allowed as a deduction all the ordinary and necessary expenses paid or incurred during the taxable year in carrying on any trade or business. An expense is ordinary if it is a customary or usual expense made by many taxpayers involved in the same business activity. An expense is necessary if it is appropriate and helpful to the taxpayer's business, even if it is not necessary in the strictest sense. In most situations, an expense that is ordinary will also be considered necessary. In addition, the expense must be business related. This means that the activity must be engaged in with the intent and expectation of making money and that there be an element of regularity and continuousness in the taxpayer's participation in the activity.

2. Although business expenses are generally deductible, the Code describes certain payments that are specifically nondeductible. Among these are payments in violation of any federal law or of any state law that is generally enforced and subjects the payer to either a criminal penalty or the loss of a license or privilege to engage in a business. Examples of nondeductible illegal payments are bribes to government officials or expenses paid in the conduct of an illegal business, such as drug trafficking.

3. Certain expenses of a political nature are nondeductible. These include:

   - expenses in connection with influencing legislation
   - expenses for participation in a political campaign on behalf of or in opposition to a candidate for public office
   - expenses for influencing public opinion on a political issue
   - expenses for communication with certain executive branch officials to influence their official positions

   Note that expenses for influencing legislation at the local level are not subject to this rule and are therefore deductible. Also, if the taxpayer is a professional lobbyist who is paid to influence legislation, he or she may deduct expenses related to that activity as business expenses.

4. A fine or penalty paid to a government for the violation of any law is nondeductible. Such payments include fines paid for tickets received in connection with speeding or parking violations while conducting business.

5. "Reasonable" compensation may be loosely defined as that amount that would ordinarily be paid to an employee for similar services by similar companies operating in similar circumstances. Under the judicial decisions on this issue (of which there are many), several factors are taken into account in making the factual determination of reasonableness. These factors include (but are not limited to):

   - the degree and nature of the employee's responsibility in his or her position (including responsibility for the production of profits)
   - the amount the employee could have earned in similar employment for another company
   - the salary paid in prior years for the same services
   - the time the employee devotes to the performance of the services
   - the nature of the services and any unique or peculiar abilities of the employee in rendering those services
   - the amount of salaries paid to other employees providing similar services who are not shareholders
   - general economic conditions in the region

The employee's total compensation is considered in determining reasonableness, including commissions, overrides, bonuses, and payments to pension, profit-sharing, or 401(k) plans.

6. Answers:

   a. One special rule limiting deductions for compensation applies only to payments by publicly held corporations. The general definition of "excessive employee remuneration" is remuneration paid to a "covered employee" that is in excess of $1 million for the taxable year.

   b. A "covered employee" is either one of the following:

      - the chief executive officer of the corporation or an individual acting in such capacity at the close of the taxable year
      - one of the four most highly paid officers of the corporation for the taxable year (other than the chief executive officer)

      Under this definition, the rule of excessive employee remuneration applies to no more than five employees of a company for any taxable year.

7. Treasury regulations deal with the question of whether expenses for education that is related to a business activity are deductible as business expenses. Such expenses are deductible if they meet either of the two following criteria:

   - The expenses are deductible if incurred primarily for the purpose of meeting the requirements of the taxpayer's employer or of local law as a condition for the taxpayer's retention of employment.
   - The expenses are deductible if incurred primarily for the purpose of maintaining or improving skills needed by the taxpayer in his or her current employment or business activity.

   The $500 that Don paid for tuition to attend an income tax seminar is deductible under the second criterion listed above. Don is trying to maintain or improve his skills as a tax attorney. Also, it is possible that the state in which Don practices law has a continuing education (CE) requirement that he must meet in order to maintain his law license. If this is the case, then the $500 is also deductible under the first criterion listed above.

8. The deductible percentage is now 100 percent. (This is an "above-the-line" deduction in computing AGI.)

9. Car expenses may be deducted in one of two different ways. The taxpayer may claim a standard mileage allowance for business transportation. This allowance is deemed to include depreciation, fuel, insurance, repairs, and other normal operating expenses. The only actual expenses that are deductible in addition to the mileage allowance are those for highway tolls, parking charges, and interest payments with respect to the car that are otherwise deductible under the tax law. Taxpayers who lease their cars may generally use the mileage allowance, but it must be used for the entire lease period. The mileage allowance can be claimed only with respect to those miles actually driven for business purposes.

   In lieu of claiming the standard mileage allowance, taxpayers may claim their actual expenses (including depreciation) in using a car for business. Any depreciation deductions will be limited by that percentage of the overall use of the car that represents business use. Cars used for business are also subject to special "luxury auto" limits on depreciation. Repairs made to the car will also be deductible only to the extent of the percentage of business use. The "actual expense" method requires significant recordkeeping to substantiate deductions. Many taxpayers find it easier to simply keep a log of business miles, and claim deductions under the standard mileage allowance.

Taxpayers who lease a car used for business are not permitted to claim depreciation for the car, since the required ownership does not exist. However, such taxpayers are permitted to deduct their lease payments to the extent the car is used for business if the standard mileage allowance is not used. This deduction is, however, subject to an "add-back" rule. Depending on the car's fair market value, a specified amount of the lease payment must be included in the taxpayer's gross income to offset part of the lease payment deduction. This rule corresponds to the "luxury auto" limitations that apply to taxpayers who claim depreciation for the business use of a car. These add-back amounts are relatively low and are published annually by the IRS to reflect adjustments for inflation.

10. A taxpayer is generally considered to be "away from home" on a trip if the taxpayer stays overnight or longer at a temporary business location.

11. Answers:
    a. Since George Collins's trip is primarily for business, his lodging cost at the Plaza is deductible.
    b. His travel expenses to New York and back are also deductible since the trip is primarily for business.
    c. The cost of garaging the car is deductible. The servicing expenses are also deductible as costs of maintaining and operating a car used in Collins's trade or business. However, Collins could elect to take the standard mileage rate approved by the IRS in lieu of his actual operation costs.
    d. These expenses are not deductible. They are not directly attributable to Collins's business, even though the trip is primarily for business.
    e. Business phone calls are deductible as an ordinary and necessary business expense.
    f. These expenses are deductible since the taxi fares are directly attributable to Collins's business.

12. In order for an entertainment expense to be deductible, it must be "ordinary and necessary," plus it must also be either "directly related to" or "associated with" the active conduct of the trade or business. Moreover, the taxpayer must be able to substantiate the entertainment expenditures with adequate records of the business-related event or with other sufficient corroborating evidence.

13. Answers:
    a. Goodwill expenses associated with the conduct of business are entertainment expenses to promote goodwill. Such goodwill entertainment expenses often are incurred in an effort to obtain new business or to encourage the continuation of existing business relationships.
    b. Goodwill entertainment expenses may be deductible if the expenses directly precede or follow a bona fide business discussion. "Directly preceding or following" has been interpreted in the regulations to mean that the entertainment occurs on the same day as the business discussions. However, entertainment expenses that occur on a day other than the day of business discussions may still qualify for deduction depending on the facts and circumstances.

14. The primary purpose of any combined business and entertainment activity must not be a social one, but one to further the taxpayer's business. In order for Dwayne's expenses for taking Eddie to the basketball game to be deductible, the entertainment activity (that is, attending the basketball game) must be directly related to or associated with the active conduct of the trade or business of being an auto parts distributor.

In the scenario presented in the question, Dwayne's expenditures fail the "directly related" requirement. Dwayne is not actively engaged in a business negotiation or discussion with Eddie and the expenditures are not made in a clear business setting. Moreover, since Dwayne did not discuss business with Eddie either before or after the game, the expenditures also fail the "associated with" requirement. Therefore, Dwayne will not be able to deduct his expenses for the game as business entertainment expenses.

15. Deductions for all business meal and entertainment expenses are limited to 50 percent of the amount that is deductible after taking into account all other limitations and restrictions. Because of this limitation, the after-tax cost of business meals and entertainment is higher than it would be otherwise. For example, if the total cost of entertainment is $100 and the whole amount is deductible, the after-tax cost for a taxpayer in the 28 percent bracket would be $72 (.28 × $100 = $28; $100 − $28 = $72). However, with a 50 percent limitation on the amount that is deductible, the after-tax cost of entertainment will increase to $86 (.28 × $50 = $14; $50 − $14 = $36; $50 + $36 = $86).

16. Deductions for expenses paid or incurred in connection with the operation and maintenance of an entertainment facility are generally disallowed. No depreciation deductions may be taken even when a facility is primarily used for business entertainment. Out-of-pocket expenses for entertaining at a facility, such as the cost of food and beverages, fall within the general entertainment rules.

    Deductions for tickets to entertainment events that qualify as business expenses are limited to the face value of the tickets. The face value limitation will make the premium paid to a scalper, as well as the premium paid to a legitimate ticket agency, nondeductible. The deduction, of course, is then further reduced by the 50 percent limitation.

17. No portion of Gwen's membership fee to the country club is deductible. However, business entertainment expenses incurred while using the club may be deductible, subject to the 50 percent limitation.

18. Deductions for tickets to entertainment events that qualify as business expenses are limited to the face value of the tickets. Therefore, the $100 premium paid by Frosty Forrest is nondeductible. Moreover, the $100 face value for the pair of tickets must be further reduced by the 50 percent limitation. Consequently, only $50 of the original $200 paid by Frosty for the tickets is deductible as a business entertainment expense.

19. The deduction for business gifts that are ordinary and necessary business expenses is limited to $25 per donee. Thus, only $25 of each $40 gift given by Nancy Sellers to her employees is deductible.

20. Entertainment expense deductions will be disallowed unless the taxpayer can adequately substantiate the deductible expenses. This requires the taxpayer either to maintain an account book or diary in which the expenditures are recorded at or near the time of expenditure or to substantiate the deductions with other sufficient evidence. The use of an account book is the better way to meet the substantiation requirements, and it must include the following:

    - the amount of each expenditure
    - the date of the entertainment and its duration
    - the place of the entertainment, including name and address
    - the business purpose
    - the business relationship, meaning the name, title, or other description of the person entertained, sufficient to establish a business relationship to the taxpayer

    If entertainment is merely "associated with" the taxpayer's business, then the taxpayer must record the place and duration of the business discussion and must identify the persons entertained who participated in the discussion.

Lodging expenses and other expenses of $75 or more require documentary evidence, such as a receipt, to support the deduction. Incidental items, such as taxi fares or telephone calls, may be aggregated on a daily basis.

21. Answers:

    a. Although John Curley has incurred ordinary and necessary entertainment expenses directly related to his business, he cannot deduct these expenses unless he can substantiate the expenses by adequate records.

    b. A box full of receipts is not considered to be adequate record keeping. The taxpayer should maintain a diary where he records (at or near the time of the expenditure) the (1) amount of the expenditure, (2) date and operation, (3) place of entertainment, (4) business purpose, and (5) business relationship. If a diary is not kept, corroborating evidence will be required on audit.

    c. Records should be made at or near the time when expenditures are incurred.

22. "Production of income" expenses are deductible by individual taxpayers. These are expenses that are paid in the course of an activity that is engaged in for profit but does not rise to the level of a business activity. The Code states that such deductible expenses must be "ordinary and necessary expenses paid or incurred during the taxable year." They must fall within one of the three following categories:

- expenses made for the production or collection of income. An example of such an expense would be the costs of managing stock and bond investment and trading activities (but not the actual cost of an investment or an expense taken directly from the proceeds of a sale).
- expenses for the management, conservation, or maintenance of property held for the production of income. An example of this type of expense would be expenses for repair and maintenance of a rental property owned by the taxpayer.
- expenses made in connection with the determination, refund, or collection of any tax. An example of this type of expense would be the fee paid by an individual for the preparation of his or her income tax return or for representation at a tax return audit.

23. Answers:

    a. An investment counselor's fee for advice on stocks and bonds is a deductible nonbusiness expense. This type of expense is clearly related to an activity engaged in for profit and is an example of an expense for the production or collection of income.

    b. An investment counselor's fee for advice on apartment house management is a deductible nonbusiness expense. This type of expense is clearly related to an activity engaged in for profit and is an example of an expense for the management, conservation, or maintenance of property.

    c. An attorney's fee for drafting a simple will is a nondeductible expense because it is essentially personal in nature.

    d. An attorney's fee solely for advice as to the tax consequences of contemplated income and estate tax planning is a deductible nonbusiness expense. This type of expense is an example of an expense made in connection with the determination, refund, or collection of taxes.

24. Lord Skidrow's expenses in defending a lawsuit challenging his title to the apartment building are not deductible as nonbusiness expenses. The costs of acquiring, perfecting, or defending a taxpayer's legal title to property are part of the capital investment in the property and therefore do not qualify as current nonbusiness expenses. Such costs may be recovered for tax purposes when the property is sold or depreciated.

25. Even though the employee uses the office regularly to promote the employer's business, it is not used exclusively as an office. Therefore the employee would not be entitled to claim a deduction for home-office expenses.

26. There are two primary considerations in determining whether a home office is a "principal place of business." They are:

    - the relative importance of the activities performed at each location of the business conducted in the home office
    - the relative amount of time spent at each location

    However, even if these two considerations are not otherwise satisfied, a taxpayer may still qualify for a home-office deduction under the principal place of business requirement if the newer "administrative or management activities" rule is met. The principal place of business test can be passed if the taxpayer uses the home office for "administrative or management activities," and there is no other fixed location where the taxpayer performs a substantial portion of such activities for the business conducted in the home office.

27. All deductions allocable to the business activity, including both deductions otherwise allowable as personal expenses (i.e., allocable mortgage interest expense and real estate taxes) and business deductions not attributable to the home office, must be subtracted from the gross income of the business conducted in the home office to determine the amount of home office deductions that will then be allowable. As a result, the remaining home office deductions (excluding mortgage interest expense and real estate taxes) can reduce the business activity's income to zero, but can not create a loss. Excess home office deductions can be carried over to future years and applied against business income under the same test.

28. Answers:

    a. No deductions attributable to rental use are allowed since Jim Real actually rented the home for less than 15 days during the taxable year.
    b. The $1,000 rental income is excludible from Jim's gross income because the home was rented for less than 15 days during the taxable year.

29. Miscellaneous itemized deductions that are not subject to the 2 percent floor include:

    - impairment-related work expenses of a handicapped taxpayer
    - the deduction for estate tax related to income in respect of a decedent
    - deductions related to personal property used in a short sale
    - deduction for the restoration of the amount held under claim of right
    - deduction for annuity payments ceasing before the taxpayer's recovery of investment in the contract
    - amortizable bond premiums
    - cooperative housing costs
    - gambling losses to the extent of gambling winnings

# Self-Test Answers for Chapter 7

1. True.
2. True.
3. False. There are certain expenditures that are not deductible because to allow them would be against public policy. Included in this category are fines or similar penalties paid to a government for a violation of a law as well as illegal bribes and kickbacks.
4. True.
5. False. The deduction is disallowed when the taxpayer's adjusted gross income exceeds a specified amount based on filing status.
6. True.
7. True.
8. False. Although the guests were mostly business customers, the expense would be denied because the event was not related to the taxpayer's trade or business.
9. False. The deduction would be denied because the setting was such that there was little or no possibility of engaging in the conduct of business. Discussions at nightclubs, theaters, or sporting events are not generally considered "directly related" to the business, but may qualify if a business discussion took place before or after the event (under the "associated with" requirement).
10. True.
11. False. The deductible amount for tickets is limited to the face amount only, subject to the 50 percent limitation. There is no deduction allowed for any premiums paid.
12. False. Country club dues are not deductible.
13. True.
14. True.
15. True.
16. False. Deductions are generally available for an office at home only if the taxpayer uses the office exclusively for business.
17. False. Home-office deductions (excluding mortgage interest expense and real estate taxes) are not permitted to the extent they create or increase a net loss from business activities. Disallowed deductions may be carried over and deducted in succeeding years subject to the same limitations.
18. True.
19. False. The deduction for unrecovered basis in an annuity is a miscellaneous itemized deduction that is not subject to the 2 percent floor.
20. True.

# Chapter 8

## Answers to Review Questions

1.  The general rules that must be satisfied to claim a loss deduction are:

    - the loss must be suffered by the taxpayer who is claiming the deduction
    - the loss must result from an identifiable event
    - the property that is the subject of the loss must have had a determinable monetary value
    - there must be economic substance to the loss, and not just the form of a transaction that appears to result in a loss
    - a loss of an expected economic benefit or item of income is not a deductible loss

2.  A loss deduction is allowable for property that has become worthless. However, the taxpayer must be able to show that there was an identifiable event that resulted in the worthlessness of the property. The deduction cannot be taken for property that merely decreases in value. The property must become completely worthless in order for a change in value to result in a deductible loss without a sale or exchange. A loss deduction may also arise from the abandonment of property. If the owner of the asset acts affirmatively and with manifest intent to abandon the property, the amount of the taxpayer's adjusted basis in the property is generally deductible as a loss.

3.  The Code specifies that a deduction is allowed for losses "not compensated for by insurance or otherwise." This means that deductions are allowed only to the extent that the loss is not otherwise compensated for. If there is no insurance, the loss is deductible if it otherwise meets the loss deduction requirements. If the loss is partially compensated for by insurance or through some other arrangement, the portion of the loss not compensated for is deductible.

4.  Answers:

    a.  For business entities, such as corporations and partnerships, losses are generally deductible in the year when they occur if the loss meets the overall requirements for deductibility. No special restrictions on losses generally apply to these entities.

    b.  Individual taxpayers may claim loss deductions if the loss is incurred in the course of a trade or business or in the course of any transaction entered into for profit. If a loss does not fall into either of these categories, it is a personal loss for income tax purposes. Personal losses are deductible only if they are theft losses or casualty losses (losses arising from fire, storm, shipwreck, or another type of casualty). In other words, an individual's losses that result from a business or profit-seeking activity are deductible subject to the same rules that apply to a business entity. Other losses are nondeductible except for theft and casualty losses.

5.  Answers:

    a.  Tony is entitled to deduct the purchase price of his new machine, $500, as a business loss.

    b.  The loss of an estimated $5,000 worth of business is not deductible. The Code requires that the loss be of capital, not just expected income. Tony's "loss" of business is not the loss of capital with an ascertainable value. It is merely his estimate of what might have occurred if the answering machine had been in operation.

    c.  Although the automobile accident was Tony's fault, the loss may be deductible as a casualty loss since it was not intentional. The computation of the casualty loss is as follows:

| Loss ($50,000 – $20,000) | $30,000 |
|---|---|
| Minus $100 reduction | ( 100) |
| | 29,900 |
| Minus 10% of adjusted gross income | ( 25,000) |
| | $4,900 |

    d.  Although Tony realized a loss by selling his house for $200,000 less than he paid for it, he cannot deduct a loss for income tax purposes. Losses from the sale of private residences are nondeductible personal losses.

    e.  Tony saw in the newspaper that his stock had declined in value by $1,000, but unless he actually sells the stock—and realizes a loss—he is not entitled to any deduction. There has been no identifiable event.

6.  The term casualty may be generally defined as damage, destruction, or loss occurring to a taxpayer's property as a result of a sudden, unusual, or unexpected cause.

    Fires, storms, shipwrecks, accidents, floods, freezes, and earthquakes are examples of sudden and unexpected events that result in casualty losses. Normal wear and tear of property, and even gradual damage to property resulting from undiscovered causes, are not events that result in deductible personal casualty losses.

    Since the damage to Kathy's house occurred over a period of time and therefore was not sudden, she is not eligible for a casualty loss deduction.

7.  Mr. T's deductible loss would be the lesser of the van's adjusted basis or the difference in its fair market value before and after the loss. Therefore, the deductible loss would be $7,000, the difference in the van's value before and after the accident. The van was not completely destroyed, so Mr. T cannot deduct the full amount of his basis since that is larger than the difference in value.

8.  A more generous tax deduction is allowed for business bad debts as compared with nonbusiness bad debts. Business bad debts are deductible in full from the taxpayer's ordinary income, while nonbusiness bad debts are specifically characterized by the Internal Revenue Code as short-term capital losses. Therefore nonbusiness bad debts are subject to the limitations on deductions for capital losses. In most cases, worthless debts owed to business entities will be characterized as business bad debts. Corporations do not have nonbusiness bad debts.

    The characterization of a bad debt as a business or nonbusiness bad debt is determined by reference to the nature of the creditor's activity in lending the money and not by reference to the purpose for which the borrower used the funds.

9.  Answers:

    a.  A business bad debt must be one of the following:

- a debt that is created or acquired (as the case may be) in connection with the taxpayer's trade or business
- a debt in which the worthlessness of the debt is incurred in the taxpayer's trade or business

    Neither one of these situations characterizes the $10,000 loan by Marjorie to her friend Tommy. Since Marjorie is neither in the business of lending money nor is the money lent for the purpose of improving the business relationship with Tommy, the bad debt should be treated as a nonbusiness bad debt.

    b.  The Code specifies that a bad debt deduction is allowed for a debt which becomes worthless within the taxable year. The debt must become worthless for a deduction to be allowable, and it must be claimed for the tax year in which worthlessness occurs.

    c. Bill's payment on the guarantee will result in his being able to take a nonbusiness bad debt deduction. The payment on a guarantee will result in a business bad debt deduction only if the guarantor had entered into the loan arrangement in the course of a business activity. Bill, as Tommy's accountant, is not in the business of guaranteeing loans and consequently is not eligible for a business bad debt deduction. However, even though Bill's guarantee was not actually part of his accounting business, there was nonetheless a profit motive in making the guarantee, and under these circumstances Bill's payment on the guarantee will result in a nonbusiness bad debt deduction and short-term capital loss treatment.

10. The Code specifies that when a business bad debt (but not a nonbusiness bad debt) is recoverable only in part, a deduction may be allowed for the part of the debt that becomes worthless during the tax year. In other words, a deduction may be claimed for partial worthlessness of a business debt.

11. When a bad debt for which a deduction was legitimately claimed in an earlier tax year is repaid unexpectedly, the taxpayer who claimed the deduction must include the amount of the repaid debt in gross income to the extent that the previous deduction of the debt produced a tax benefit.

12. The loss from a nonbusiness bad debt is deductible as a short-term capital loss. However, since an individual's net capital losses are only deductible against ordinary income up to $3,000 per year ($1,500 if married filing separately) while business bad debts are deductible in full against ordinary income, the tax treatment of nonbusiness bad debts is significantly less favorable than that which applies to business bad debts.

13. Answers:

    a. Under these circumstances, the payment on the guarantee will result in a business bad debt deduction.

    b. Under these circumstances, the payment on the guarantee will result in a nonbusiness bad debt deduction and short-term capital loss treatment.

    c. Under these circumstances, the payment on the guarantee will not result in a bad debt deduction. There must be a legally enforceable debt and a legitimate profit motive on the part of the guarantor in order for payment on a loan guarantee to result in any bad debt deduction.

# Self-Test Answers for Chapter 8

1.  False. A mere decline in value, without a realizable event, does not give rise to a deductible loss.
2.  True.
3.  True.
4.  True.
5.  False. Deductible casualty losses do not include the ordinary situation in which a taxpayer simply loses or mislays property.
6.  True.
7.  False. Nonreimbursed casualty losses are deductible to the extent (a) each loss exceeds $100 and (b) total losses are greater than 10 percent of the taxpayer's adjusted gross income. Both of these limitations must be applied.
8.  True.
9.  True.
10. False. Bad debts owed to a corporation are not treated as nonbusiness bad debts.
11. True.
12. True.

# Chapter 9

## Answers to Review Questions

1. Answers:

   a. If a capital expenditure is made for an asset that is eligible for cost recovery, the cost of the asset may be deducted over a number of tax years, but not, as a general rule, fully deducted in the year the expense is made. One important exception to this rule applies if the taxpayer acquires property that is eligible for the first-year expense election under Code Sec. 179.

   b. First, if the outlay is for the acquisition of property that has a useful life of more than 1 year, the outlay will be considered a capital expenditure. Second, if the outlay is for the enhancement or improvement of an asset the taxpayer already owns, it will be treated as a capital expenditure, provided it either enhances the value of the property or results in an improvement with a useful life of more than 1 year. In other words, a capital expenditure is considered to be a new investment in property, while a current expense is more akin to a repair or a maintenance item that is necessary for the operation or well-being of a property or asset that the taxpayer already has. Current expenses are deductible on a taxpayer's current income tax return; capital expenditures typically are deductible over a number of tax years.

2. The general rule regarding the deductibility of personal expenses is that they are disallowed. Nonetheless, certain personal expenses are expressly deductible under the Code in spite of the general rule of disallowance.

3. Answers:

   a. Homeowners insurance premiums are nondeductible personal expenses.
   b. Personal life insurance premiums are nondeductible personal expenses.
   c. Commuting expenses for traveling to and from the office are nondeductible personal expenses.
   d. Expenses for groceries and utilities are nondeductible personal expenses.

4. Nonreimbursed medical expenses (including amounts paid for medical insurance as well as prescription drugs and insulin) incurred primarily for the prevention or treatment of physical or mental defects or illness are deductible in the year paid to the extent they exceed 7.5 percent of adjusted gross income for taxpayers who are 65 at the close of the tax year. The taxpayer may add all his or her medical care expenses and calculate the total deductible amount as follows:

| | |
|---|---:|
| Drugs | $ 300 |
| Nonreimbursed doctor and hospital expenses | 569 |
| Insurance premium | 3,000 |
| Total nonreimbursed medical expenses | $3,869 |
| Minus 7.5% floor | ( 3,000) |
| Amount deductible | $ 869 |

Note: if the taxpayer had not reached 65 during the tax year, none of the expenses would be deductible since the floor is 10 percent, not 7.5 percent of AGI.

5. Special restrictions apply to expenses for cosmetic surgery. Such expenses are deductible only if the surgery is done to correct a condition resulting from an accident, a congenital abnormality, or a disfiguring disease. Expenses for surgery performed to

improve the appearance of an individual, such as a face lift procedure or similar surgery, do not qualify for the deduction. The question in evaluating the deductibility of cosmetic surgery is whether the procedure either meaningfully promotes the proper function of the body or prevents or treats illness or disease.

6.  One principle that the IRS will generally follow in determining whether a given expense qualifies as a deductible medical expense is the question of whether the service, product, or activity paid for is simply for the general preservation of the individual's health or well-being or rather is for the alleviation or treatment of a specific disease or defect. If the expense is for something that only promotes the individual's overall general health, it will generally not be deductible. On the other hand, if a physician prescribes an activity or program of treatment to improve or correct a specific medical condition, the expense is more likely to be deductible.

7.  Qualified long-term care expenses are generally treated as medical expenses for income tax purposes, and qualified long-term care insurance premiums are also generally deductible subject to limitations.

8.  The deduction for long-term care insurance premiums is limited to a maximum dollar amount per year that varies according to the age of the person covered under the policy. The dollar limits are indexed annually for inflation and apply per covered individual rather than to each tax return.

9.  Yes, premiums for qualified long-term care insurance contracts are eligible for the above-the-line deduction for health insurance premiums paid by self-employed taxpayers.

10. Taxes not incurred in the course of a business or income-producing activity that are deductible on Schedule A by individual taxpayers include the following:

    *   state, local, and foreign real property taxes
    *   state and local personal property taxes
    *   state and local income taxes
    *   state and local general sales taxes (through 2013 ) in lieu of the deduction for state and local income taxes
    *   the generation-skipping transfer tax imposed on income distributions
    *   the environmental tax imposed by IRC Sec. 59A

    Certain other taxes are deductible, including foreign income, war profits, and excess profit taxes for taxpayers who do not claim a foreign tax credit for these taxes.

11. Yes, the IRS would challenge this deduction if Cecil were audited. Assessments for improvements are not deductible taxes.

12. The exception applies to a property owner who sells the property during the period covered by an existing assessment. In such cases, the property taxes are subject to a rule of apportionment. For deduction purposes, the taxes are treated as assessed to the seller of the property for the time period up to but not including the date of sale. As of the sale date, the taxes are treated as having been assessed to the buyer for deduction purposes. The apportionment is calculated based on the number of days of the assessment period that each party owns the property. This treatment is consistent with the usual apportionment of tax payments that appears on a closing statement or settlement sheet upon the sale of a home.

13. Five basic categories of interest payments are:

    *   interest on indebtedness incurred in the course of a trade or business ("business interest")
    *   interest on indebtedness incurred in the course of an activity entered into for profit that is not a business activity ("investment interest")

- interest on indebtedness incurred in connection with a passive activity ("passive activity interest")
- certain interest on indebtedness secured by the taxpayer's residence ("qualified residence interest")
- personal interest

14. The general rule for interest payments on indebtedness incurred in the course of a business activity is that the payments are deductible. However, notwithstanding the general rule of deductibility for business interest, there may be another set of rules that applies to the interest payment that could limit or prevent its deductibility.

15. Answers:

   a. Deductions for investment interest expenses are limited to the taxpayer's "net investment income" for the year.

   b. "Net investment income" is the excess of the taxpayer's investment income over the taxpayer's investment expenses. Investment income is the sum of gross income from property held for investment other than qualified dividends taxed at the special reduced maximum rates, plus gain other than long-term capital gain attributable to the disposition of property held for investment. Investment expenses are generally all deductible expenses (other than interest expenses) that are connected with the production of investment income.

16. Answers:

   a. "Qualified residence interest" is interest paid on a loan secured by the taxpayer's personal residence that is deductible for federal income tax purposes.

      For interest payments to be qualified residence interest, the loan must be secured by a "qualified residence." A qualified residence includes the taxpayer's principal residence plus one other residence (such as a vacation home) that the taxpayer selects to be treated as a qualified residence. Such other residence need not be a house but could include vehicles and water vessels that have sleeping and eating accommodations. If such other residence is rented by the taxpayer for part of the year, it must not qualify under the "rental use" test of the vacation home deduction limitations. If it does qualify under that test, it cannot also be a "qualified residence" for purposes of deducting qualified residence interest.

      For qualified residences, there are two types of qualified residence interest: interest paid on "acquisition indebtedness" and interest paid on "home equity indebtedness."

   b. "Acquisition indebtedness" is any indebtedness that is incurred in acquiring, constructing, or substantially improving a qualified residence and that is secured by such residence. It also includes the refinancing of such indebtedness, but only to the extent the principal amount of the refinancing does not exceed the amount of the refinanced indebtedness. Amounts refinanced in excess of the existing principal balance may qualify as home equity indebtedness.

      The maximum amount of acquisition indebtedness for any one taxpayer (including a married couple filing jointly) is $1 million. For married taxpayers filing separately, the limit is $500,000. Indebtedness in excess of these amounts will not be treated as acquisition indebtedness and will not give rise to deductible interest unless the debt qualifies as home equity indebtedness.

   c. "Home equity indebtedness" is indebtedness other than acquisition indebtedness secured by a qualified residence to the extent that:

- the total amount of acquisition and home equity indebtedness does not exceed the fair market value of the residence
- the aggregate amount of the taxpayer's home equity indebtedness does not exceed $100,000 ($50,000 for married taxpayers filing separately)

Note that the $100,000 limit (as well as the $1 million limit on acquisition indebtedness) is a per-taxpayer, and not a per-residence, limitation. Also, the total of acquisition indebtedness and home equity indebtedness may exceed the taxpayer's cost for the home but may not exceed the fair market value of the home. Finally, home equity indebtedness does not have to be used for any specific purpose in order to generate qualified residence interest. Such loans can generally be used for any purpose desired by the taxpayer.

17. In order for taxpayers to be assured that points paid upon the origination of a loan will be currently deductible, the following requirements must be met:

- The loan must be incurred in connection with the acquisition of the taxpayer's principal residence.
- The loan must be secured by the taxpayer's principal residence.
- The points must be calculated as a percentage of the principal amount of the loan.
- The points must be paid to the lender directly by the taxpayer rather than added to or derived from the principal amount of the loan.
- The lender's charging of the points must be consistent with an established business practice in the area in which the loan is made and must not exceed the amount generally charged for points in such area.
- The settlement statement describing the acquisition of the home must designate the payments as points (using terms such as points, discount points, loan origination fees, or similar terminology).

18. The general rule is that personal interest is not deductible unless it is qualified residence interest or certain interest paid in connection with a loan for higher education.

19. As a general rule of tax law, an otherwise allowable deduction for an interest payment or any other expense will be disallowed if the interest expense or other expense is incurred in the course of producing income that is exempt from income tax.

20. The Code specifically prohibits the deduction of expenses incurred in connection with the purchase of tax-exempt obligations. Thus Mrs. Temponi's

a. interest payments on the $100,000 loan incurred to purchase the bonds would not be deductible, and the
b. payment of $500 to First Investment Corporation as a fee for advice about purchasing the bonds would likewise not be deductible

21. Contributions are generally subject to a limit of 50 percent of AGI as well as an overall limitation on itemized deductions. In addition to these limits, charitable contributions must meet four other requirements to be deductible. These requirements are:

- The donee organization must be qualified.
- Property, not services, must be the subject of the gift.
- The contribution must be in excess of value received.
- The contribution must be paid in cash or other property before the close of the tax year in question.

22. Generally a charitable contribution of less than a donor's entire interest in property is nondeductible. However, gifts of a partial interest in property are deductible in the following three narrowly defined situations:

a. a gift of an undivided portion of the donor's entire interest
b. a gift of a remainder interest in a personal residence or farm
c. a gift of a partial interest if transferred in trust

23. Robert can deduct nothing. A contribution of rent-free use of property is nondeductible. A contribution of services to a charity is also nondeductible. The contribution must be of the property itself.

24. Egbert may currently deduct $50,000 (50 percent of his $100,000 adjusted gross income). The remaining $10,000 can be carried over as an excess contribution.

25. Answers:

    a. The $3,000 contribution to the needy neighbors would not be deductible, since one of the requirements for deductibility is that the charity be a qualified organization and not an individual.

    b. The $2,000 contribution to the Chamber of Commerce would not be deductible. While a Chamber of Commerce is a tax-exempt organization, it is not considered a qualified charitable organization even though it pays no income tax. Qualified charitable organizations are those that are operated exclusively for charitable, religious, scientific, literary, or educational purposes.

    c. Gladstone cannot claim a deduction for allowing a charitable organization the rent-free occupancy of his mansion. Likewise, he cannot claim a deduction for volunteering services because he has not contributed any property to a charity. However, any out-of-pocket expenses that Gladstone incurs for the conference, such as rental of chairs or heating and lighting the mansion, are tax deductible.

    d. Gladstone would obtain a $5,000 deduction for his cash contribution to the Salvation Army. His maximum deductible cash contribution to all public qualified charities can be $100,000, which is 50 percent of his $200,000 adjusted gross income. Excess contributions above $100,000 can be carried over to the 5 following tax years. Gladstone must also comply with the substantiation requirements that apply to deductible contributions of $250 or more for each such contribution. (Any monetary contributions made in cash or by check require the donor to maintain either a bank record of the contribution or written communication from the donee substantiating the contribution. Additional substantiation requirements exist if the amount of a single contribution exceeds $250.)

    e. Gladstone may deduct the full value of the stock contributed to the United Way. He will avoid taxation of the potential gain on his stock. The maximum charitable deduction for property that will give rise to long-term capital gain (such as stock) in any year is 30 percent of adjusted gross income. Gladstone's donation is less than 30 percent of his AGI of $200,000 ($60,000). Hence he may deduct the entire $20,000.

    f. Gladstone may only deduct his cost of producing the papers and letters, which in this case is $100. A taxpayer's deduction is limited to his cost for property that would result in ordinary income if sold. If Gladstone sold his papers, he would have ordinary income.

    g. Contributions to charitable organizations in foreign countries are not deductible (unless there is a reciprocal agreement with a foreign government in a tax treaty).

    h. Gladstone would not be able to deduct the present value of the remainder interest, since the trust does not qualify as a charitable remainder unitrust or charitable remainder annuity trust. A trustee's discretionary power to invade trust principal for the benefit of the noncharitable beneficiary will disqualify such a trust.

    i. Assuming that Clear Springs is a qualified public charity, Gladstone is entitled to deduct the lesser of the replacement cost of a paid-up policy (that is, the single-premium cost of a comparable contract at the donor's attained age), or the amount of his basis in the policy. No income tax deduction would be allowed if Gladstone retains ownership of the policy and merely names the charity as revocable beneficiary.

    j.  The charitable contribution deducted for this policy is limited to the lesser of the cash surrender value (interpolated terminal reserve plus unearned premium) or the net premium cost. Here Gladstone's deduction is limited to $6,800.

26. Larry Churnkey will be able to deduct 80 percent of the $1,000 donation to the university, which amounts to $800. This 80 percent provision applies to contributions made by an alumnus of a university that requires the alumnus to make the contribution in order to be eligible to purchase season tickets for the university's athletic teams.

27. Answers:

    a.  When intangible personal property or real property is given to a qualified public charity, the individual donor's deduction generally may not exceed 30 percent of his or her AGI. If the gift exceeds this percentage limitation, the donor taxpayer may carry over the deduction for up to 5 future years. The full fair market value of the gift property is generally deductible.

    b.  There is a special election that an individual donor may use to increase the 30 percent limit to 50 percent of his or her AGI. To increase the 30 percent limit to 50 percent, the donor taxpayer must be willing to reduce the value of the gift property by 100 percent of the potential gain.

        The election can be important for a donor taxpayer whose income fluctuates widely from year to year. It is of particular value when the amount of appreciation is small. Note, however, that the amount representing 100 percent of the potential gain may not be carried over and deducted in a later year if the election is made. Consequently, the deduction under the special election is limited to the donor taxpayer's basis in the property, which if not completely deducted in the current year can be carried over and deducted in a later year.

28. Answers:

    a.  *Ordinary-income property* is an asset that would have resulted in ordinary income (rather than capital gain) on the date of contribution had it been sold at its fair market value rather than contributed. Ordinary-income property includes (1) capital assets held 12 months or less at the time contributed, (2) works of art, books, letters, and similar property, but only if given by the person who created or prepared them or for whom they were prepared, and (3) a business person's stock in trade and inventory (which would result in ordinary income if sold).

    b.  Taxpayers' deductions are generally limited to their basis (cost) for ordinary-income property. For example, if a famous painter donated one of his paintings worth $25,000 to an art museum, the deductions would be limited to the cost for canvas, paint, and so forth. No deduction would be allowed for the value of the painter's efforts or reputation nor would a deduction be allowed for the fair market value of the painting. In other words, only the cost of the materials that go into producing the painting are deductible.

        One exception to this rule provides for an increased incentive to corporations to make charitable contributions of scientific equipment to colleges or universities. In this situation, the deduction is allowed in an amount equal to the cost of the property plus one-half of the unrealized appreciation limited to a maximum deduction of twice the basis of the property. There are other similar exceptions.

29. Answers:

    a. Where appreciated tangible personal property is use related, the entire fair market value at the date of the gift is deductible. In other words, a use-related gift of tangible personal property held for the requisite period is treated exactly the same as any other long-term capital-gain property. Thus the donor is subject to the 30-percent-of-AGI limitation or may elect to reduce the value of the gift by 100 percent of the potential gain realized if the gift was sold rather than contributed. By doing this, the percentage limitation on the donor's adjusted gross income ceiling would be increased to 50 percent. In some cases this would result in a larger, immediate deduction.

    b. Where appreciated tangible personal property is use unrelated, the fair market value of the gift must be reduced by 100 percent of the potential gain. By doing this, the percentage limitation on the donor's AGI ceiling is increased to 50 percent.

30. The gift of tangible personal property must be complete in the sense that all interests and rights to the possession and enjoyment of the property must vest in the charity. This means that a transfer of a future interest in property to a charity is not deductible until all intervening interests in and rights to possession held by the donor or certain related persons or organizations have expired (or unless the gift is in the form of a future interest in trust that meets certain specified requirements).

31. Answers:

    a. To qualify for a charitable tax deduction, a charitable remainder annuity trust must meet all the following requirements:

- A fixed amount or fixed percentage of the initial value of the trust must be payable to the noncharitable beneficiary.
- This annuity must not be less than an amount equal to 5 percent nor more than 50 percent of the initial fair market value of all the property transferred in trust. Further, the charitable remainder interest must be at least 10 percent of the initial net fair market value of all property placed in trust.
- The specified amount must be paid at least annually to the beneficiary out of income and/or principal.
- The trust must be irrevocable and not subject to a power by either the donor, the trustee, or the beneficiary to invade, alter, or amend the trust.
- The trust must be for the benefit of a named individual or individuals who must be living at the time the property is transferred to the trust. An amount can be paid to a person for life or for a term of years not greater than 20 years. The remainder must go to charity (charities) and cannot be split between charitable and noncharitable beneficiaries.

    If these requirements are met, the donor will be entitled to an income tax deduction limited to the present value of the remainder interest.

    b. To qualify for a charitable tax deduction, a charitable remainder unitrust must meet all the following requirements:

- A fixed percentage of the net fair market value of the principal, as revalued annually, must be payable to the noncharitable beneficiary. Therefore the amount payable to the income beneficiary may fluctuate from year to year.
- The percentage payable must not be less than 5 percent nor more than 50 percent of the annual value. For most transfers in trust, the value of the charitable remainder interest must be at least 10 percent with respect to the net fair market value of each contribution.

- The unitrust may provide that the noncharitable beneficiary can receive the lesser of (1) the specified fixed percentage or (2) the trust income for the year, plus any excess trust income to the extent of any deficiency in the prior years by reason of the limitation to the amount of trust income in such years.
- The noncharitable income beneficiaries must be living at the time of transfer in trust, and their interests must be for a term not exceeding 20 years or for their respective lives.
- The entire remainder must go to charity (or charities).

If these requirements are met, the donor will be entitled to an income tax deduction limited to the present value of the remainder interest.

c. To qualify for a charitable tax deduction, a pooled-income fund must meet all the following requirements:

- The donor must contribute an irrevocable, vested remainder interest to the charitable organization that maintains it.
- The property transferred by each donor must be commingled with the property transferred by other donors.
- The fund cannot invest in tax-exempt securities.
- No donor or income beneficiary can be a trustee.
- The donor must retain a life income interest for himself or herself or one or more named income beneficiaries.
- Each income beneficiary must be entitled to and receive a pro rata share of the income (annually) based on the rate of return earned by the fund.

If these requirements are met, the donor will be entitled to income and gift tax deductions. The economic advantage to the donor of making this transfer is that the donor is obtaining diversification for the income beneficiary without incurring the capital-gains tax that would ordinarily be imposed if the donor exchanged securities for other securities.

32. Life insurance is a favored means of making charitable contributions for several reasons:

- The death benefit going to charity is guaranteed as long as premiums are paid.
- Life insurance provides an amplified gift that can be purchased on the installment plan.
- Life insurance is a self-completing gift.
- The death proceeds can be received by the designated charity free of federal income and estate taxes, probate and administrative costs and delays, brokerage fees, or other transfer costs.
- Because of the contractual nature of the life insurance contract, large gifts to charity are not subject to attack by disgruntled heirs.
- A substantial gift may be made with no attending publicity.

33. Answers:

a. When the value of the policy (interpolated terminal reserve plus unearned premium on the date of the gift) exceeds the policyowner's net premium payments, the deduction for a gift of the policy is equal to the policyowner's basis (cost), that is, the net premium payments paid by the policyowner.

b. When the policyowner's net premium payments exceed the value of the policy, the deduction for a gift of the policy is equal to the policy's value.

c. The charitable deduction allowed for a paid-up or a single-premium policy is the lesser of the policy's replacement cost or the policyowner's basis. The replacement cost of a single-premium or paid-up policy is the single premium the same insurer would charge for a policy of the same amount at the insured's attained age (increased by any dividend credits and reduced by any loans).

   d. The maximum charitable deduction allowed for a newly issued policy is the gross premium paid by the policyowner.

34. Answers:

   a. Rev. Rul. 2009–13 determined that a life insurance policy is a capital gain asset. If a life insurance policy is surrendered at a gain, the gain is taxed as ordinary income to the extent of the inside buildup of the policy and capital gain to the extent of the excess (if any) over the inside buildup. . The amount of the charitable deduction for Sidney's gift will be the fair market value of the policy reduced by the ordinary income element (the inside buildup) had the policy been sold. Capital gain property gifted to a public charity is subject to the 30 percent-of-AGI limitation.

   b. Even though the amount of net premiums paid by Sidney exceeds the policy's paid-up value, his charitable contribution for the policy gift is limited to the policy's replacement cost.

# Self-Test Answers for Chapter 9

1. True.

2. False. Generally, a capital expenditure must be capitalized rather than expensed. However, any applicable cost recovery deduction may be taken in the year of acquisition.

3. False. Subject to certain limited exceptions, personal expenses are nondeductible. Most expenditures that are normal in the course of maintaining a household are considered nondeductible personal expenses.

4. False. Premiums paid by the policyowner-insured for personal life insurance are generally not deductible.

5. False. A medical expense deduction is allowed for the entire portion of deductible medical expenses (including medical expense insurance) that exceeds the applicable floor of the taxpayer's adjusted gross income.

6. True.

7. True.

8. True.

9. False. Qualified long-term care insurance premiums are eligible for treatment as medical expenses. However, deductibility of these premiums is subject to annual dollar amount limitations based on the covered individual's age.

10. True.

11. False. Taxes assessed for local benefits that tend to increase the value of the property assessed are not deductible. Assessments for streets, sidewalks, and other improvements would fall within this category. These expenses must be treated as capital expenditures that are added to the cost of the property.

12. True.

13. True.

14. False. A combination of "acquisition indebtedness" and "home equity indebtedness" can produce fully deductible interest payments even though the total indebtedness on the taxpayer's principal residence exceeds the taxpayer's cost (but not the fair market value) of the residence.

15. True.

16. True.

17. True.

18. True.

19. True.

20. False. A taxpayer may only deduct as a charitable contribution the amount contributed in excess of the value received. Therefore if the dinner was worth $15 and the taxpayer made a contribution of $25, $10 would be deductible.

21. False. No deductions are allowed for gifts made to foreign charities, except where allowed by treaty.

22. False. A contribution of a rent-free occupancy or the right to use property is not deductible as a charitable contribution.

23. True.

24. True.

25. False. Individuals may deduct contributions annually in amounts up to 50 percent of their contribution base (adjusted gross income) for gifts to qualified public charities.

26. True.

27. False. A use-related property is deductible at its fair market value on the date of the gift. However, if the gift is use-unrelated, the deduction is limited to the donor's basis in the property.

28. True.

29. True.

30. False. A charitable contribution deduction for a premium-paying policy is limited to the lower of the cost of the contract (net premiums paid) or the value of the policy.

# Chapter 10

## Answers to Review Questions

1. The current amount of the credit is $1,000 per qualifying child.

2. The otherwise allowable credit is phased out by $50 for each $1,000 (or fraction thereof) by which modified AGI exceeds the threshold amount. The phaseout begins at the following levels of modified AGI:

   | | |
   |---|---:|
   | Married filing joint return | $110,000 |
   | Married filing separately | 55,000 |
   | Unmarried taxpayers | 75,000 |

3. Answers:

   a. For adoptions of children without special needs, the amount of the credit depends on the amount of qualified expenses. The maximum amount of the credit per eligible child is $12,970 for 2013. No more than the maximum amount may be claimed for any one child regardless of the number of years for which the credit is claimed for that child. In other words, the limit on the credit is a cumulative limit per child.

   b. The full adoption credit is now allowed to taxpayers who adopt a special needs child regardless of the amount of qualified adoption expenses paid by the taxpayer. This means that taxpayers will be eligible for the maximum allowable credit even if they have little or even no actual adoption expenses.

4. The adoption credit is phased out for taxpayers whose AGI for the year 2013 exceeds $194,580. To calculate the amount of the credit that is phased out, divide the amount of the taxpayer's AGI in excess of $194,580 by $40,000. Then multiply the resulting percentage by the otherwise allowable amount of the credit. The credit is completely phased out when AGI reaches $234,580.

5. Answers:

   a. A qualifying individual must fall within one of the following definitions:

      - the taxpayer's "qualifying child" who is under the age of 13
      - an individual who is physically or mentally incapable of caring for himself or herself and is also the taxpayer's dependent for tax purposes
      - the taxpayer's spouse who is physically or mentally incapable of caring for himself or herself

   b. There is a limit on the amount of expenses that can be counted in calculating the allowable credit. For taxpayers caring for one qualifying individual, the maximum amount is $3,000 per year.

6. It is important to know how the American opportunity tax credit (formerly the Hope scholarship credit) and the Lifetime learning credit interact with one another.

   First, the credits cannot be claimed together with respect to the education expenses of the same student. Similar to the Hope scholarship credit, the American opportunity tax credit applies on a per-student basis, while the Lifetime learning credit applies on a per-taxpayer basis. This means that the American opportunity tax credit applies separately with respect to each student for whom the taxpayer pays education expenses, while the Lifetime learning credit applies on an overall basis to all qualifying expenses (for one or more students for whom the Hope or American credit is not claimed) paid by a given taxpayer. If a taxpayer elects the American opportunity tax credit for the college expenses of one child, he or she may still elect the Lifetime learning credit for the qualifying education expenses of another child or children. Alternatively, the American opportunity tax credit can be elected separately for each child in college. As previously indicated, however, the Lifetime learning credit cannot be elected with respect to expenses that have been claimed under either the American opportunity tax credit or former Hope scholarship credit.

7. Answers:

   a. Both credits are available with respect to qualified tuition and related expenses. Such expenses include those paid for attendance at a postsecondary educational institution offering credit toward a degree or other recognized credential. They do not include expenses for courses involving sports, games, or hobbies unless the course is part of the degree program. Room and board, transportation, and living expenses are also not qualified expenses for these credits.

   b. The Hope scholarship credit is allowed only for expenses incurred during the first two years of the student's postsecondary education and can be elected for only 2 taxable years for any one student. The student must carry at least one-half the normal full-time workload for the course of study being pursued. It is calculated based on 100 percent of the first $2,000 of qualifying expenses and 25 percent of the next $2,000 of expenses. The expense limits are indexed for inflation.

   The American opportunity credit is available for all four years of postsecondary education and adds course materials to "qualifying expenditures." In addition, the credit is 100 percent of the first $2,000 of qualifying expenses, and 25 percent of the next $2,000 in qualifying expenses.

   c. Unlike the Hope scholarship credit and current American opportunity tax credit, the lifetime learning credit may be claimed for all postsecondary years of education expenses, including graduate and professional school expenses. It is also available with respect to expenses of a student who is taking courses to acquire or improve job skills, even if that student is not a half-time student as required under both the Hope credit and American opportunity rules. It is equal to 20 percent of the first $10,000 of qualifying expenses paid by the taxpayer for the year.

8. The allowable American opportunity/Hope scholarship and Lifetime learning credits are phased out proportionately for taxpayers with modified AGIs in excess of certain levels, which are adjusted annually for inflation. To calculate the amount of the credit that is phased out, divide the amount of the taxpayer's modified AGI within the phaseout range by the amount of the phaseout range. Then multiply the resulting fraction by the allowable credit. The credit is completely phased out when the fraction reaches 1. However, the American opportunity tax credit phases out at significantly higher levels of AGI than both the Hope scholarship and lifetime learning credits.

# Self-Test Answers for Chapter 10

1. False. The child must be under age 17, not age 19.
2. True.
3. True.
4. True.
5. True.
6. False. Taxpayers may receive an additional credit for a second child, but not for more than two children.
7. False. The credit may currently be claimed in an amount not exceeding $2,500, per student on an annual basis.
8. True.

# Chapter 11

## Answers to Review Questions

1.  Four basic conditions are necessary for the allowance of cost recovery deductions:

    - The asset must be either used in the taxpayer's business activity or held for the production of income.
    - The taxpayer must have an ownership interest in the asset.
    - The taxpayer must have a depreciable basis in the property.
    - The asset must be considered to have a limited useful life.

2.  Methods used for computing a depreciation deduction for property placed in service before 1981 include:

    - the straight-line method, under which the taxpayer simply divides the depreciable basis in the property by the number of years of the property's applicable recovery period to arrive at an annual deduction that remains the same over the course of the recovery period
    - the declining-balance method, under which a fixed percentage of the taxpayer's original basis in the depreciable property is allowed in the first year. In the following year, the same percentage is applied to the basis of the property as adjusted to that point. In other words, this method applies the same percentage to the property's basis each year as adjusted for previous depreciation claimed. The percentage used cannot be more than twice the percentage used in applying the straight-line method to the original basis of property in the year it is placed in service.
    - the sum-of-the-years-digits method, under which a changing percentage is applied to the basis of the property to calculate allowable depreciation. This percentage is determined by using a fraction, the numerator of which is the number of years remaining in the cost recovery period as of the year the depreciation is being claimed. The denominator of the fraction is the sequential sum of the numbers representing each year in the total recovery period of the property. In each successive year of the recovery period, the numerator of the fraction will change but the denominator will not. The fraction for each year is applied to the original basis of the property and not to the basis as adjusted for depreciation.
    - any other consistent method under which the first two-thirds of the depreciable asset's recovery period does not result in cost recovery greater than that obtainable under the declining-balance method. Other such methods include the "unit-of-production" and "machine hours" methods.

3.  The concept of claiming deductions for depreciation is based on the premise that taxpayers should be able to deduct, or recover for tax purposes, the amount of an investment in an income-producing asset over the period of time that the asset is useful for its intended purpose. A rule related to the useful life concept requires that the basis of depreciable property be reduced by the amount of depreciation allowable for a given year. This means that if the taxpayer omits a depreciation deduction for a certain asset from a tax return in a given year, the basis of the asset will still be adjusted over the term of its recovery period in a systematic way that corresponds to a systematic use of the asset.

4.  Answers:

    a.  A deduction for obsolescence becomes available at the point in time when the taxpayer can determine with reasonable certainty that the asset has or will become obsolete. At that time, the taxpayer's remaining basis in the asset may be deducted ratably between the time when obsolescence becomes reasonably certain and the time of actual obsolescence.

  b. Obsolescence is not always related to the physical condition of the asset. It occurs when an asset becomes economically useless to the taxpayer who owns it. This could be the result of technological or scientific advances in a given business or industry, through changes in applicable laws that essentially prohibit the use of the asset, or simply because of changes in economic conditions that remove profitability from the use of the asset.

5. ACRS applied to depreciable assets placed in service between January 1, 1981, and December 31, 1986. MACRS generally applies to assets placed in service after December 31, 1986. In addition, ACRS and MACRS are substantially different with respect to both the recovery periods and the recovery methods assigned to specific types of assets. ACRS generally provides for faster cost recovery than does the current MACRS system.

6. The property "classes" or applicable recovery periods for MACRS are as follows:

- 3-year property. This property class includes most racehorses, tractors, breeding hogs, certain manufacturing tools, qualified rent-to-own property, and certain computer software that is readily available to the public.
- 5-year property. This class includes cars, most trucks, computers, copiers, typewriters, solar and wind energy equipment, breeding and dairy cattle, and semiconductor manufacturing equipment.
- 7-year property. This class includes office furniture and fixtures, most machinery and industrial equipment, and railroad equipment.
- 10-year property. This class includes property used in petroleum refining, fruit-bearing trees and vines, and barges, tugboats, and other water transportation vessels.
- 15-year property. This class includes telephone distribution plants, service station buildings, pipelines, billboards, and such land improvements as roads, sidewalks, and bridges.
- 20-year class. This class includes certain farm buildings and municipal sewers.
- 27½-year class. This important class of property includes residential real estate.
- 39-year class. This class includes nonresidential rental property, such as office buildings, factories, and warehouses. If the property was placed in service before May 13, 1993, the recovery period is 31½ years.

7. Answers:

  a. Assets in the 3-, 5-, 7-, and 10-year recovery classes are generally depreciated under the double- (or 200 percent) declining-balance method with a switch to the straight-line method at the point where the straight-line method produces a higher deduction.

  b. Property in the 27½-year, 31½-year, or 39-year recovery classes is depreciated under the straight-line method. This includes all real estate, both residential and nonresidential.

8. Answers:

  a. 7-year class

  b. double-declining-balance method, with a later switch to straight line (MACRS Table)

  c. 5-year class

  d. double-declining-balance method, with a later switch to straight line (MACRS Table)

9. A mid-month convention is used for real estate. Depreciable real estate placed in service (or disposed of) during any month of the taxable year is treated as being placed in service (or disposed of) in the middle of that month in calculating allowable depreciation.

10. Elective alternatives available under MACRS are as follows:

   - Taxpayers may elect the straight-line method of depreciation for classes of property that are eligible for the declining-balance method. The straight-line method is then used over the property's MACRS recovery period.
   - An alternative depreciation system (ADS) allows taxpayers to elect the 150 percent declining-balance method for certain property otherwise eligible for the 200 percent declining-balance method, or to elect the straight-line method for property otherwise eligible for the 150 percent declining-balance method. Under this ADS election, such property is generally depreciated over a recovery period longer than its MACRS recovery period.

11. Major differences between ACRS and MACRS involve the following types of property:

   - automobiles. Under ACRS, autos were depreciated over a 3-year period using a recovery rate similar to the 175 percent declining-balance method. Under MACRS, autos are in the 5-year class of property.
   - office furniture, fixtures, equipment, and heavy machinery. Under ACRS, these assets were depreciated over a 5-year period using a 175 percent declining-balance method. Under MACRS, these assets are depreciated over 7 years, although the 200 percent declining-balance method applies.
   - real property. Under ACRS, depreciable real estate was recovered over a 15-, 18-, or 19-year recovery period depending on the date the property was placed in service. Real estate was also eligible for an accelerated method of depreciation corresponding to the 175 percent declining-balance method. Under the current MACRS, real property is depreciated using the straight-line method over a recovery period of 27.5 years (residential) or 39 years (nonresidential).

12. Answers:

   a. All depreciation claimed for tangible personal property is generally subject to recapture on the sale of the property regardless of the depreciation method used. This means that gain from the sale of the property will be taxable as ordinary income to the extent of the cumulative depreciation deductions claimed for the property.

   b. Only real estate that has been depreciated under an accelerated method will be subject to depreciation recapture. The amount of depreciation recaptured depends on whether the property is residential or nonresidential real property. For residential property, only that amount of depreciation claimed that is in excess of the amount allowable under the straight-line method is recaptured. For nonresidential property, there is generally recapture of the full amount of depreciation unless the straight-line method is elected for the property. For real estate acquired and placed in service after December 31, 1986, only the straight-line method of depreciation is allowed. However, although recapture does not technically exist, a special 25-percent capital gain rate applies to "unrecaptured Sec. 1250 gain" or "unrecaptured depreciation," meaning all of the depreciation allowed or allowable may be subject to a tax rate of 25 percent (and not the preferential long-term capital gain rate of 20 percent).

13. Answers:

a.  Taxpayers other than trusts, estates, or certain noncorporate lessors may elect to deduct or "expense" the full cost of certain depreciable property in the year such property is placed in service. This election generally applies only to depreciable tangible personal property that is acquired by purchase for active use in the taxpayer's trade or business. Real estate does not qualify for the "expensing election." Also, other depreciable property not used in a trade or business (that is, investment property) does not qualify.

b.  The maximum dollar amount eligible for expensing is reduced by one dollar for each dollar of the cost of qualifying property in excess of a specified amount as adjusted for inflation (or legislation) that the taxpayer places in service during the taxable year.

In addition, the amount of the expensing allowance for any year is also limited by the taxpayer's taxable income derived from the business for the year (determined without regard to the expensing election). Any amount disallowed under this limitation may be carried forward to future tax years.

14. Any amount claimed under the expensing election must be subtracted from the taxpayer's depreciable basis; that is, a taxpayer cannot claim both expensing and depreciation with respect to the same dollars of capital investment.

15. If such property is not used more than 50 percent for business purposes, depreciation of the property must be computed under the MACRS alternative depreciation system (ADS). This means that straight-line depreciation must be used over the applicable ADS recovery period. For computers, the ADS recovery period is 5 years.

The amount eligible for cost recovery of any asset is limited to the percentage of the cost of the asset that corresponds to the percentage of its business use. If such business use is not more than 50 percent, expensing of such assets under IRC Sec. 179 is effectively prohibited because of the requirement that ADS depreciation be used.

16. The dollar amount limitations on cost recovery for luxury autos apply to both depreciation deductions and the first-year expensing election. The limits are indexed annually for inflation. If the dollar limitations result in the taxpayer having unrecovered basis in the vehicles after the normal 5-year recovery period is over, the maximum amount for the fourth year can be claimed in succeeding taxable years until the vehicle is fully depreciated. Note that these amounts are maximum amounts. If the vehicle is not used 100 percent for business (and for the production of income), the dollar amount limitations are applied before the percentage reduction in allowable depreciation that reflects the percentage of personal use is applied. This ensures that vehicles used partially for personal purposes will not be eligible for 100 percent of the dollar amount limitations. Different rules apply to certain vehicles, including those with gross vehicle weight of over 6,000 pounds.

17. The following intangible assets are eligible for cost recovery through amortization:

-   the goodwill of a business
-   the "going concern" value of a business
-   a company's "workforce in place," including its composition and terms and conditions of its employment
-   business books and records, information bases, and operating systems (but not computer software available for public purchase and subject to a nonexclusive license)
-   patents and copyrights acquired in a transaction involving an acquisition of an interest in a business
-   formulas, processes, designs, know-how, and similar property

- licenses, permits, or other rights granted by a governmental unit
- franchises, trademarks, and trade names
- a covenant not to compete entered into in connection with an acquisition of an interest or a substantial portion of an interest in a trade or business

18. Qualifying intangible assets may be recovered ratably over a 180-month period. The amortization calculation is similar conceptually to the calculation under the straight-line method of depreciation.

# Self-Test Answers for Chapter 11

1. True.
2. True.
3. False. Depreciation deductions may be taken only by the equitable owner of property, not by the mortgagee.
4. False. The cost of land is not depreciable.
5. True.
6. True.
7. True.
8. False. Obsolescence means a loss of economic usefulness from abnormal causes rather than the ordinary physical wear and tear on the property.
9. True.
10. True.
11. True.
12. False. Automobiles can generally be depreciated on a double-declining-balance basis (using MACRS Tables) over 5 years.
13. True.
14. False. The half-year convention is used for all property classes other than real property and certain intangible assets. The recovery deduction for real property is based on the month of the first year that the property was placed in service. The convention used for intangible assets is also based on the month of acquisition.
15. True.
16. True.
17. False. The Sec. 179 election generally applies to depreciable tangible personal property that is acquired and used only in the taxpayer's trade or business. Property acquired and held for the production of income does not qualify for the Sec. 179 election.
18. True.
19. False. The expensing election is only available for certain property used in a trade or business.
20. False. The dollar limits apply annually to cost recovery deductions. If these limits do not allow the full depreciation percentage to be taken, the recovery period is extended to allow cost recovery later.
21. True.

# Chapter 12

## Answers to Review Questions

1. The passive activity rules of Sec. 469 were enacted because Congress was concerned with the availability of substantial tax "losses" (deductions in excess of income) claimed by taxpayers with respect to business activities in which the taxpayer owns an interest but does not substantially participate in on a regular and continuous basis. The most common examples of such activities include rental activities (particularly rental real estate) and the ownership of limited partnership interests and similar types of business ownership. The rules were designed to reduce losses of tax revenues resulting from so-called "tax shelters."

2. Answers:

   a. "Portfolio income" includes dividends, interest, royalties, income from annuities, and the gain or loss realized from the disposition of property that generates portfolio income for the taxpayer. It would also include gain or loss realized from the disposition of property held for investment, even if the property was not income producing. Portfolio income does not include any income generated in the conduct of a business.

   b. "Active income" includes wages and other compensation generated by the efforts of the taxpayer. It essentially depends on whether the taxpayer has materially participated in the activity generating the income.

   c. "Passive income" is the income remaining after a taxpayer's portfolio income and then active income has been segregated. Income from a business entity in which the taxpayer does not materially participate in the activity of the entity would be characterized as passive income.

3. An individual taxpayer who actively participates in a rental real estate activity may deduct up to $25,000 of losses from the activity against nonpassive income. The $25,000 amount is phased out by 50 percent of the amount by which the taxpayer's adjusted gross (with certain modifications) income exceeds $100,000. "Active" participation under this exception requires less participation than the general rule of "material" participation.

# Self-Test Answers for Chapter 12

1. True.
2. True.
3. False. The taxpayer must own at least 10 percent of the rental real estate, measured by value.

# Chapter 13

## Answers to Review Questions

1. To determine realized gain or loss on the sale or other disposition of an asset, it is first necessary to ascertain the amount realized from the sale or exchange as well as the taxpayer's basis in the transferred asset.

    The "amount realized" is simply the value of all property received in exchange for the asset transferred. This would be the amount of any money received for the property, plus the fair market value of any other property received as consideration for the property transferred.

    The taxpayer's "basis" in the property transferred (or "adjusted basis" as referred to in IRC Sec. 1001) is generally the taxpayer's cost for the property, subject to certain adjustments. These adjustments may include reductions in basis for previously claimed depreciation deductions, or increases in basis for additions or improvements that the taxpayer made to the property.

    The taxpayer's basis in an asset must be known to calculate the amount of realized gain or loss upon the sale of the asset as well as the amount of any depreciation or other cost recovery deductions available with respect to that asset. Once the amount realized and the taxpayer's adjusted basis in the property have been determined, realized gain or loss is calculated by subtracting the adjusted basis from the amount realized in the sale or exchange.

2. Answers:

    a. Realized gain may be described as the economic gain that a taxpayer obtains from the sale or exchange of property. As a general rule, any gain *realized* on the sale or exchange of property must also be *recognized* for federal income tax purposes; that is, it must be included in the taxpayer's gross income for the year it is realized.

        Any income a taxpayer realizes is includible in gross income unless some provision of the Code specifically states otherwise. The Code does contain several provisions that define exchanges of property in which realized gain does not have to be recognized for tax purposes.

    b. When an exchange of property does not result in current recognition of gain, the gain realized is not altogether eliminated but merely deferred until the taxpayer disposes of the property received in the exchange. This deferral of realized gain is accomplished largely through the mechanism of a "substituted" basis, under which the taxpayer transfers his or her basis in the old property over to the newly acquired property rather than obtain a cost or fair market value basis in the new property. In this way, any untaxed gain in the old property is preserved in the new property and will be recognized when the new property is sold in a taxable transaction.

3. Answers:

    a. Janet's basis in the shares is $25,000 ($50 × 500).
    b. The total amount realized by Janet on the sale of the shares is $50,000 ($25,000 × 2).
    c. The total gain realized by Janet is $25,000 ($50,000 – $25,000).

4. Answers:

    a. Rocksalt's basis for the Apex stock he receives in the exchange is $15,000.
    b. Rocksalt's gain on the exchange is $5,000 ($15,000 – $10,000).

5. The taxpayer receiving the gift (the donee) generally has a basis equal to that of the same property in the hands of the taxpayer making the gift (the donor). This basis rule may be referred to as a carryover basis.

6. A taxpayer receiving property as compensation for services will have a basis in the property equal to its fair market value at the time it was received.

7. If a taxpayer purchases property and takes (or assumes) a mortgage on the property to finance its purchase, the taxpayer's basis in the property is equal to its entire cost, including the amount subject to the mortgage.

8. If the taxpayer can adequately identify the actual shares being sold, then the basis of those specific shares can be used as his or her basis in calculating realized gain or loss.

9. Answers:

    a. The $9,000 airplane is taxable income received as compensation.
    b. The sale of the airplane generates a $3,000 gain ($12,000 – $9,000).

10. Answers:

    a. If the property is includible in the gross estate of the decedent for federal estate tax purposes, the taxpayer receiving the property takes a basis in the property equal to its fair market value as of the date of the decedent's death.
    b. If the fiduciary of the decedent's estate elects the so-called "alternate valuation date" (6 months from the date of death) for the valuation of property for federal estate tax purposes, then the taxpayer takes a basis equal to the fair market value of the property at that time.

11. The portion of jointly owned property that is includible in a decedent's gross estate is eligible for a fair market value adjustment. Therefore the surviving joint tenants receive a basis step-up (or step-down if the property has experienced a reduction in value) to fair market value for the portion of the property that was includible in the decedent's gross estate.

12. If the decedent acquired property in his or her estate as a gift within 1 year of death, and if the donor of the gift to the decedent is the same person (or that person's spouse) to whom the property passes from the decedent's estate, the basis step-up will not be available.

13. If a taxpayer receives property by means of a gift made during the donor's lifetime, a carryover basis rule applies. With respect to gifted property, the donee's basis is computed by reference to the property's adjusted basis in the hands of the donor. An additional basis rule applies to gifted property—if the donor paid gift taxes in connection with the donative transfer, an adjustment to the carryover basis is made.

14. Answers:

    a. As a result of the carryover basis rule for gifted property, the gain realized upon a subsequent sale of the property by the donee will be equal to the amount realized on the sale minus the donee's carryover basis in the property (as adjusted for any gift tax attributable to appreciation at the time of the gift).
    b. A special basis rule applies in order for a donee's sale of property received by gift to result in a realized loss for income tax purposes. In calculating a realized loss resulting from such a sale, the donee's basis will be the lower of the carryover basis received by the donee, as adjusted, or the property's fair market value at the time of the gift (not at the time of the sale).

15. The general rule is that property acquired by gift in the hands of the donee has the same basis as it had in the hands of the donor. In this case Lynne's basis was $1,000, and that is the basis Jim takes; so his gain on the sale is $2,000 ($3,000 – $1,000).

16. For purposes of determining loss, the basis of the property in the hands of the donee is (1) the donor's basis or (2) the fair market value of the property at the time of the gift, whichever is lower. The fair market value at the time of the gift is $5,000, which is lower than the donor's basis. Therefore Bob has a $500 loss ($5,000 − $4,500).

17. Basis adjustments that may be required for various types of property include:

    - adjustments for cost recovery and related types of deductions claimed with respect to the property
    - adjustments for permanent improvements to property made after the taxpayer acquires the property
    - various adjustments that are made to the basis of a taxpayer's ownership interest in a business as a result of distributions, proportionate shares of the business entity's income or loss, and other items

18. Answers:

    a. The general concept behind the like-kind exchange rules is that where a taxpayer uses an exchange to continue an investment in a specific type of income-producing property but needs a different piece of such property from that which was needed before, the continuation of what is essentially the same investment in the same type of property should not give rise to a taxable event.
    b. Property eligible for the like-kind exchange provisions includes domestic real estate, machinery, equipment, vehicles, office furniture, computers, and most other real and personal property that would typically be used for income-producing purposes. It must be understood that one type of qualifying property cannot be exchanged for another type of qualifying property. The qualifying properties must be of generally the same type; that is, they must be of "like kind."
    c. If the taxpayers taking part in an exchange are related persons, generally each taxpayer must keep the property for 2 years after the date of the exchange. If one of the parties to the exchange sells the property received in the exchange before the 2-year period is up, both the selling party and the other party to the exchange will have a taxable event.

19. Answers:

    a. In a like-kind exchange, often cash or other property will be involved in the exchange along with the like-kind property to make the total of the value of property surrendered in the exchange equivalent to the total of the value of property received. In such an exchange, the cash or other property that is not property of like-kind is referred to as "boot."
    b. The inclusion of boot in a like-kind exchange does not disqualify the exchange from tax-deferred treatment. However, it does result in the exchange being treated as partially taxable. Note that the taxpayer who pays the boot property will not have to recognize gain or loss on an otherwise qualifying exchange. However, the taxpayer who receives the boot property must recognize any realized gain but only to the extent of the value of the boot received. Also note that no loss will be recognized by the taxpayer (only gain) as a result of the receipt of boot in the exchange.

20. There are basis adjustments that must be made to the substituted basis of the taxpayer in cases where the exchange does not solely involve property of like-kind. The required basis adjustments fall within two general categories:

- The taxpayer's basis must be decreased by the amount of any money and/or the value of any other "boot" property received in the exchange, or increased by the amount of any such property paid in the exchange.
- The taxpayer's basis must be increased by the amount of any gain that was recognized on the exchange or decreased by the amount of any loss recognized on the exchange. The Code provides for a basis decrease for any loss recognized on an exchange even though a realized loss is not permitted to be recognized as a result of the receipt of boot in a partially taxable exchange.

21. Answers:

    a.  Neither party has any gain or loss to recognize upon the exchange of the buildings, since their exchange is of a like-kind investment property. The basis in the new building for each party is the basis in their old building. This is known as a substituted basis.

    b.  If both were dealers and traders of buildings, the nonrecognition provisions would not apply. Both Sam's business loss and Carol's gain would be recognized.

    c.  If Sam or Carol receives cash in the deal, then the exchange is not solely in kind-it is a boot transaction.

        (1) If Sam receives cash, he is taking a loss on the deal. He realizes $77,000 in the exchange, but his basis is $80,000. No loss is recognized in like-kind exchanges where boot is received.

        (2) On the other hand, if Carol receives cash, she has a gain of $27,000 ($77,000 – $50,000) but recognizes it only to the extent of boot received. Hence, Carol would recognize $2,000.

    d.

        (1) Sam's basis in the new building is the basis of his old property ($80,000) decreased by the amount of money received ($2,000), or $78,000.

        (2) Carol's basis in the new property is the basis of her old property ($50,000) decreased by the amount of money received ($2,000) and increased by the amount of gain recognized in the exchange ($2,000), or $50,000.

22. The Code provides that no gain or loss will be recognized for income tax purposes upon the exchange of one life insurance, endowment, or annuity contract for another life insurance, endowment, or annuity contract.

    What this means is that a life insurance contract may be exchanged for another life insurance contract, an endowment contract, or an annuity contract. An endowment contract may generally be exchanged for another endowment contract or for an annuity contract, but not for a life insurance contract. An annuity contract may be exchanged without recognition of gain only for another annuity contract and not for a life insurance or endowment contract.

23. Answers:

    a.  Yes, no gains will be recognized from this exchange.

    b.  No, any gains will be recognized from this exchange.

    c.  No, the insurance contracts must be on the life of the same insured.

24. Answers:

    a.  The policyowner takes the same basis in the new contract as he or she had in the old contract. If the policyowner makes an additional premium payment for the new contract (which is permissible), the basis will then be increased.

b.  If the policyowner receives cash or other property pursuant to an exchange that otherwise qualifies under Sec. 1035, the policyowner will have to recognize gain in the old policy to the extent of the "boot" received in the exchange. The payment of cash by a policyowner in an exchange does not constitute the receipt of boot.

25. In general, to claim the exclusion, the taxpayer must have owned and used the home as a principal residence for an aggregate time period of 2 years out of the 5-year period immediately preceding the home's date of sale.

26. Answers:

    a.  $500,000 is the maximum amount of the exclusion.
    b.  $250,000 is the maximum amount of the exclusion.

27. If the taxpayer fails to fully meet the ownership and use rules or the "once every 2 years" rule for claiming the exclusion, and the sale of the home is due to a change of the taxpayer's place of employment, a change of health, or other "unforeseen" circumstances, the $250,000 or $500,000 maximum amount (whatever amount would otherwise be available if the taxpayer fully met the requirements) is reduced. The maximum exclusion is multiplied by the ratio of the amount of time that the taxpayer's qualifying period of ownership and use bears to 2 years. The resulting figure is the maximum amount of gain that the taxpayer is permitted to exclude from gross income.

28. Answers:

    a.  The purpose of this provision is to prevent a tax-avoidance technique in which a taxpayer could (in the absence of the wash sale rule) sell stock, claim a tax loss from the sale, then quickly repurchase the same stock so that the taxpayer's economic position regarding the stock is essentially unchanged, but a tax savings is generated.
    b.  Taxpayers are not permitted to recognize a realized loss from the sale of corporate stock or other securities if the same stock or security is repurchased by the taxpayer within a 30-day period beginning before or ending after the sale in which the loss was realized.

# Self-Test Answers for Chapter 13

1. True.

2. False. Realization of gain does not always trigger immediate taxation. The gain that is realized must be recognized for tax purposes in order to have an immediate tax effect reportable in the current taxable year. Gain that is realized but not recognized may be excluded or deferred to some later time.

3. False. The amount realized is the value of all cash or property received for the asset transferred. Realized gain is calculated by subtracting the transferred asset's basis from the amount realized.

4. True.

5. True.

6. False. When recognition of gain or loss on an exchange is postponed to a future time, the property received takes a substituted basis.

7. True.

8. True.

9. False. When property is acquired subject to a mortgage, the taxpayer's basis becomes the entire cost of the property, consisting of the taxpayer's equity plus the amount of the mortgage.

10. False. A taxpayer who receives property from a decedent receives a new basis stepped up to the fair market value of the property on generally either the date of the decedent's death or the alternate valuation date (6 months after death) if that date is elected by the executor for federal estate tax purposes.

11. True.

12. True.

13. True.

14. False. An exchange of stock for an auto of equal value is not a qualifying transaction under the like-kind exchange provisions. Therefore the gain on such an exchange is recognized to the extent of the gain realized.

15. True.

16. False. When like-kind property is exchanged for other like-kind property plus cash, the transaction is partially taxable, and gain must be recognized to the extent of the lesser of cash (boot) received or the realized gain.

17. True.

18. False. Insurance contracts are eligible for tax-free exchanges subject to certain restrictions. A life insurance contract may be exchanged for another life contract or an endowment or an annuity contract. However, an annuity contract can only be exchanged for another annuity contract. An annuity contract cannot be exchanged tax free for a life insurance contract.

19. False. Taxpayers may treat nursing home stays as "use" of their principal residence for up to 1 year of the 2-out-of-5-year use requirement. Therefore a nursing home stay does not disqualify a taxpayer from the exclusion.

20. True.

21. False. The wash sale rules aim to prevent a taxpayer from using a loss from a wash sale as part of a strategy to reduce the tax on realized capital gains.

# Chapter 14

## Answers to Review Questions

1.  The tax treatment of capital gains has long been a social, political, and economic issue in the United States. Some observers believe that capital gains should not be taxed at all on the grounds that such gains are often attributable only to inflation, or on the grounds that appreciation of a capital asset held for investment is an accretion of wealth that should not be intruded on by the government. Other observers believe that capital gains are merely one type of economic income, that there is nothing unique or special about such gains, and that they should be taxed under the same rules as ordinary income, such as wages and salaries. For the most part, however, Congress has taken a path somewhere in the middle ground of these two opposites poles, taxing capital gains but providing more lenient treatment for such gains than that which is applicable to ordinary income.

2.  There is generally a maximum tax rate of 20 percent applicable to most long-term capital gains of individual taxpayers. This maximum rate may be higher or lower depending on the type of asset involved and the income level of the taxpayer.

3.  Answers:

    a.  Under Sec. 1221 of the Internal Revenue Code, a capital asset is defined as any property the taxpayer owns (whether or not connected with a business activity) except for certain types of property specifically excluded from the definition.

    b.  The following types of property are specifically excluded by the Code from the definition of a capital asset are:

        *   "stock in trade" (that is, inventory) of the taxpayer or other property held by the taxpayer primarily for sale to customers in the ordinary course of the taxpayer's business
        *   depreciable or real property used in the taxpayer's trade or business
        *   a copyright; a literary or artistic composition; a letter or memorandum; or similar property held either by the creator of the property, or by a taxpayer whose basis in the property is determined in whole or in part by the creator of the property, or by (in the case of a letter or memorandum) the taxpayer for whom the property was prepared or produced.
        *   accounts or notes receivable acquired in the ordinary course of business for services rendered or the sale of inventory or inventory-type property and supplies of a type regularly used or consumed in the ordinary course of a trade or business.
        *   publications of the United States government that are held by a taxpayer who did not purchase the publication or by a nonpurchasing transferee (i.e., a gift) of such a taxpayer

            Note that musical compositions or copyrights in musical works held by the creator(s) of the work or by a taxpayer whose basis in the work is determined by reference to its basis in the hands of the creator(s) can now be treated as a capital asset.

4.  In order for gain with respect to an asset to be taxed, there must be a realization of gain. In the case of a capital asset, realization of gain generally occurs through a sale or a taxable exchange of the asset.

5.  Sales of capital assets held by an individual for more than 12 months are generally eligible for the maximum rate of 20 percent on long-term capital gains. Sales of capital assets held for 12 months or less are treated as short-term capital gains and are subject

to ordinary income tax rates, unless the short-term gains are offset by capital losses. For lower bracketed taxpayers, the rate of taxation on long term capital gains is either 15 or zero percent. These two lower rates apply to taxpayers whose incomes fall below $450,000 for joint filers and surviving spouses, $425,000 for heads of household, and $400,000 for single filers.

6. For corporations, capital losses are deductible only against capital gains. If capital losses exceed capital gains for the year, the corporation will have a capital loss carryover.

   For individuals, capital losses are fully deductible against capital gains for the year. If the individual has both short-term and long-term capital gains and/or losses, there are specific procedures for the netting of those gains and losses. If the individual has only capital losses and no capital gains, or if, under the netting procedures, the individual's capital losses exceed capital gains for the year, the capital losses may be deducted from the individual's ordinary income in an amount up to $3,000 per year. If such net capital losses exceed $3,000, the excess may be carried forward to future tax years by individual taxpayers until the excess losses are used up. For married taxpayers filing separately, the $3,000 capital loss limitation is reduced to $1,500.

7. The steps in the netting process are as follows:

   - Any short-term capital gains and losses are netted together to determine the amount of the taxpayer's net short-term capital gain or loss.
   - Any long-term gains and losses from the sale of "collectibles" (the gain from which would be taxed at a maximum rate of 28 percent) are netted together to determine the taxpayer's net "collectibles" gain or loss.
   - The portion of any long-term gains from the sale of real estate attributable to unrecaptured depreciation (the gain from which would be taxed at a maximum rate of 25 percent) are added together to determine the taxpayer's total gain in this category.
   - Long-term gains and losses from the sale of capital assets (the gain from which would generally be subject to the 15 percent maximum tax rate) are netted together to determine the taxpayer's net long-term capital gain or loss in this category.

     After the gains and losses have been separated into these various baskets and netted against each other, there are additional netting procedures if one or more of the baskets contains a net capital loss. However, if there are only capital gains in the separate baskets there is no additional netting, and each category of capital gains is taxed at its applicable rate.

     If the taxpayer has net capital loss in any of the original netting baskets, the following additional netting steps apply:
   - Any net long-term loss from collectibles is netted against any net 25 percent gain first, then against any net 15 percent gain. If the collectibles loss still has not been fully utilized, the balance may be netted against the taxpayer's net short-term capital gain for the year. Any remaining loss would be deductible against ordinary income subject to the $3,000 limitation.
   - A net long-term capital loss from the sale of assets that would result in 15 percent gain if sold at a gain is handled in basically the same way: the excess loss is netted first against any net 28 percent gain, then against any net 25 percent gain, then against any net short-term capital gain. Any remaining loss would be deductible against ordinary income subject to the $3,000 limitation.
   - Any net short-term capital loss is first netted against gains subject to the maximum rate of 28 percent ("collectibles" gain), then to gains subject to the maximum rate of 25 percent, then to gains subject to the maximum rate of 15 percent (or zero

percent rate, if applicable). In other words, net short-term capital losses are netted against the capital gains subject to the highest rates first.

8. Depreciable or real property used in the taxpayer's trade or business is a special type of property for tax purposes that is treated under the rules of Code Sec. 1231. On the sale or exchange of such property, gain will be treated as long-term capital gain and loss will be treated as ordinary loss.

9. The building owned by Billy Bob is a Sec. 1231 asset. If Billy sells the building this year at a loss and it is Billy's only sale or exchange of property during the year, the loss will be deductible from Billy's ordinary income without regard to the capital loss limitations.

10. To determine the proper tax treatment for the sale or exchange of an asset, the asset must be properly classified by the taxpayer. Generally assets fall into one of three categories. Capital assets, the first category, will be subject to the rules applicable to capital gains and losses. Sec. 1231 assets, the second category, will receive long-term capital-gains treatment for net gains (subject to the recapture rule) and ordinary loss treatment for net losses. The third category is all other assets, and they will result in ordinary income or ordinary loss if sold. Since the tax treatment for the sale or exchange of an asset differs between the categories, it is necessary that an asset be correctly classified before the tax consequences of its sale or exchange can be determined.

11. Effective in 2013, a 3.8 percent "net investment income" tax applies to taxpayers whose MAGI exceeds the threshold amounts. The tax is imposed on the lesser of (1) net investment income or (2) the excess of MAGI over the applicable amount.

# Self-Test Answers for Chapter 14

1.  False. A capital asset as defined in the Internal Revenue Code includes all property held by the taxpayer whether or not it is connected with the taxpayer's trade or business, with certain exceptions. Some of the exceptions are: stock-in-trade or other property held primarily for sale to customers in the ordinary course of the taxpayer's business; depreciable or real property used in the taxpayer's trade or business; and accounts receivable acquired in the ordinary course of business for services rendered or from the sale of inventory.

2.  True.

3.  False. The gain on collectibles is subject to a maximum capital-gains rate of 28 percent.

4.  True.

5.  True.

6.  False. The maximum annual amount of net capital losses that can be deducted against ordinary income is $3,000 ($1,500 if married filing separately).

7.  True.

8.  True.

9.  False. On the one hand, if depreciable real property used in a trade or business (Sec. 1231 property) is sold and the gains exceed the losses, the resulting net gain is treated as a long-term capital gain. On the other hand, if the losses exceed the gains, the resulting net loss is treated as an ordinary loss, deductible in full from the taxpayer's ordinary income. However, net Sec. 1231 losses are subject to a special recapture provision.

10. True.

11. True.

12. False. Individuals are subject to a tax of net investment income for each year of 3.8 percent imposed on the lesser of (a) net investment income or (b) the excess of modified adjusted gross income over the threshold amount. It is possible for taxpayers to have identical modified adjusted gross income yet have differing amounts of net investment income. Consider the example of two couples filing jointly with identical modified adjusted gross income of $325,000. However, they may pay different amounts of net investment income tax because they have differing amounts of net investment income. Thus each couple will pay a differing amount of net investment income tax.

# Chapter 15

## Answers to Review Questions

1. The alternative minimum tax, or AMT, is a separate method of calculating income tax liability. It is often referred to as a "parallel" system of income taxation. It applies in cases where the calculation of the AMT results in a higher tax liability than the calculation of the regular income tax. The purpose of the AMT is to prevent the taxpayer from reducing his or her tax liability below reasonable levels through the use of certain tax benefits targeted by the AMT rules. Therefore, in calculating the AMT, certain tax benefits available under the regular tax rules are limited or prohibited under the AMT calculation.

2. Answers:

    a. The AMT is calculated by first determining the taxpayer's alternative minimum taxable income (AMTI). The calculation of AMTI uses the taxpayer's regular taxable income as a starting point, then makes adjustments to reflect the impact of tax-preference items including the elimination or reduction of certain deductions and/or credits and the addition of certain items of income that are excludible for regular tax purposes.

    b. In calculating the AMT, certain tax benefits available under the regular tax rules are limited or prohibited under the AMT calculation. Consequently when the AMT is calculated using different rules for these tax benefits, certain taxpayers will have a higher tax liability under the AMT calculation. Such tax benefits that are restricted under the AMT system may be loosely referred to as "tax-preference" items.

    c. After AMTI is calculated, it may be reduced by an exemption amount. The applicable exemption amount is determined by the taxpayer's filing status and is phased out for upper-income taxpayers.

3. Certain itemized deductions of individuals are permitted to be claimed as deductions in calculating AMTI. These include:

    - charitable contributions
    - casualty and theft losses
    - interest on indebtedness used to acquire or improve a qualified residence of the taxpayer
    - investment interest not in excess of qualified net investment income
    - the deduction for estate taxes attributable to income in respect of a decedent
    - medical expenses deductible for regular tax purposes. Note, however, that the deduction "floor" for medical expenses under the AMT rules is 10 percent as distinguished from the 7.5 percent floor that applies for regular tax purposes; furthermore, the overall limitation on itemized deductions does not apply in calculating AMTI.

4. Taxpayers who have used the standard deduction for regular tax purposes must add back the amount of the standard deduction in computing AMTI.

5. With respect to depreciable personal property placed in service after 1998, the 150 percent declining-balance method (switching to straight-line depreciation) must be substituted for property that qualifies for the 200 percent declining-balance method for regular tax purposes.

6. The phaseout of the AMTI exemption is determined by calculating the amount of the taxpayer's AMTI that is in excess of a specified threshold amount and then multiplying that excess by 25 percent. The resulting figure is the amount of the AMTI exemption

that is disallowed. If the amount disallowed is more than the AMTI exemption, then the exemption is zero.

7.  Answers:

    a.  For individuals, the tax rate is 26 percent on the first $179,500 of income subject to the AMT, or Tentative Minimum Taxable Income (other than long-term capital gains and qualified dividends) and 28 percent on amounts in excess of $179,500.
    b.  For corporations, the tax rate is 20 percent.

8.  Answers:

    a.  For new corporations, average annual gross receipts must not exceed $5 million.
    b.  For corporations that passed the initial test, average annual gross receipts must not exceed $7.5 million.

9.  The ACE adjustment takes into account certain items that are not treated as taxable income for regular tax purposes but are treated as so-called book income for accounting purposes. The ACE adjustment is calculated by adding to AMTI 75 percent of the amount by which the corporation's adjusted current earnings exceeds its AMTI. To avoid a circular calculation, the excess of adjusted current earnings over AMTI is computed using AMTI without regard to the adjustment. Seventy-five percent of the excess is then added to the corporation's AMTI base.

10. The ACE adjustment can potentially result in up to 75 percent of a corporation's life insurance proceeds being subject to the AMT. Using a 20 percent AMT tax rate, an effective tax rate of up to 15 percent on life insurance proceeds could result (that is, the amount of proceeds x .75 x .20 tax rate).

    Note that premiums paid on a life insurance contract reduce the ACE adjustment. Therefore premiums paid can reduce the amount of the corporation's income subject to the AMT. Correspondingly, increases in cash value of insurance contracts (as well as the receipt of death benefits) raise the adjustment.

# Self-Test Answers for Chapter 15

1. True.
2. True.
3. True.
4. False. The medical expense deduction floor for AMT purposes is 10 percent of adjusted gross income for all taxpayers regardless of age.
5. True.
6. True.
7. False. The exemption amount for purposes of calculating the AMT is a flat amount that is gradually phased out (reduced) above specified levels of AMTI.
8. False. The AMT rates for individual taxpayers are 26 and 28 percent.
9. False. The individual rates are 26 and 28 percent, while the corporate rate is 20 percent.
10. False. A corporation will lose its existing AMT exemption if its 3-year average gross receipts exceed $7.5 million.
11. True.
12. True.

# Chapter 16

## Answers to Review Questions

1. Answers:

   a. Generally, life insurance death benefits payable in a lump sum by reason of the death of the insured are excluded from the gross income of the beneficiary, regardless of whether the beneficiary is an individual or an entity.

   b. When death proceeds are held by the insurer for future withdrawal or distribution and only interest on the proceeds is paid to the beneficiary, the full interest payment is taxable. When the death proceeds being held by the insurer are finally distributed, they are paid tax free.

   c. For policies maturing by death, that portion of each payment made under the fixed-period, fixed-amount, or life income installment options representing the principal of death proceeds is received tax free, but that portion representing interest is taxable.

2. Answers:

   a. The portion of the payments representing death proceeds is received income tax free.

   b. Since Sue died before the date of enactment of the Tax Reform Act of 1986 (October 22, 1986), her widower is entitled to exclude up to $1,000 of the interest portion annually. The settlement option is not an interest-only option. The $200 of interest in excess of $1,000 per year is taxable.

3. Sue's widower is not eligible for the surviving spouse's interest exclusion because Sue died after October 22, 1986. Therefore, the $1,200 of interest is included in his income annually. The portion representing death proceeds is still received tax free.

4. Amounts received under a life insurance contract covering the life of an insured who is terminally ill are excludible from gross income as amounts payable by reason of the death of the insured if certain requirements are met. The amounts received qualify for the exclusion if paid by the insurance company or by a licensed viatical settlement provider. The exclusion does not apply if the amounts are paid to a taxpayer other than the insured if the insured is a director, officer, or employee of the taxpayer or has a financial interest in a business conducted by the taxpayer.

5. Jan's gain is computed as follows:

   | | |
   |---|---:|
   | Amount realized | $53,000 |
   | Minus basis ([$2,300 – $40 – $20] × 20) | ( 44,800) |
   | Gain (ordinary income) | $ 8,200 |

6. Answers:

   a. Bones would be taxed this year on the entire gain of $22,000 ($70,000 - $48,000).

   b. Bones would be taxed on the payments under the annuity exclusion ratio, which was discussed in chapter 5, since he elected the installment option within 60 days of the maturity date.

   c. Bones would be taxed this year on the entire $22,000 gain since he allowed the 60-day period after maturity to lapse without electing the installment option.

   d. Bones would be taxed this year on the entire $22,000 gain since the interest-only option must be signed before the maturity date in order to defer taxation on the gain.

7.  Where the primary payee is receiving a life income settlement and dies during a period of guaranteed payments, the contingent beneficiary will have no taxable income until the total amount received, when added to the amount that was received tax free by the primary payee, exceeds the investment in the contract. Thereafter the full amount of each payment will be taxed as ordinary income.

8.  Answers:
    a.  The general rule with respect to the income tax treatment of life insurance premiums is that they are a personal expense and as such are not deductible. The rule applies whether the premium is paid by the insured, the beneficiary, or the policyowner.
    b.  Premiums paid on business life insurance generally are not deductible.

9.  No, the premiums are not deductible by the Glimmer Corporation because it is the beneficiary and owner of the policy on the life of Richards, its president. In this regard, the Code states that no deduction shall be allowed for premiums on any life insurance policy if the taxpayer is directly or indirectly a beneficiary under the policy or contract.

10. Where a policy transferred by assignment or otherwise for a valuable consideration matures by reason of death, the transferee will be liable for income tax on the amount of death proceeds in excess of the actual value of the consideration paid for the contract plus the total of net premiums and other amounts subsequently paid by the transferee.

11. Answers:
    a.  Bull Corporation will be liable for income tax on the amount of death proceeds in excess of the consideration (cash value) paid for the policy plus the total of net premiums (and other amounts) subsequently paid by Bull Corporation. The fact that Ralph works for Bull Corporation as an account executive has no bearing since it is not one of the exceptions to the transfer-for-value rule.
    b.  This policy transfer falls under one of the exceptions to the transfer-for-value rule. Therefore, the full death proceeds will be income tax free to Leonard's designated beneficiary even though the policy was transferred for a valuable consideration.
    c.  Bonnie will be liable for income tax on the amount of death proceeds in excess of the consideration paid for the policy plus the total of net premiums subsequently paid by Bonnie. The fact that Bonnie has an insurable interest in Sharon has no bearing on Bonnie's liability for income taxes.
    d.  Both Quint and Clint will be liable for income tax on the amount of death proceeds in excess of the consideration paid for the policy plus the total of net premiums subsequently paid by each. The transfer of a policy from an insured who is a shareholder in a closely held corporation to a fellow shareholder is not one of the exceptions to the transfer-for-value rule.

12. The five specified exceptions to the transfer-for-value rule are:
    *   transfers to the insured
    *   transfers to a partner of the insured
    *   transfers to a partnership in which the insured is a partner
    *   transfers to a corporation in which the insured is a shareholder or an officer
    *   transfers in which the transferee's basis in the transferred policy is determined in whole or in part by reference to the transferor's basis

13. Answers:
    a.  The concept of insurable interest specifies that in order to obtain insurance on the life of another, there must be a reasonable expectation of benefit or advantage to the applicant from continuation of the life to be insured or an expectation of loss or

detriment from the cessation of that life. Lacking the requisite of insurable interest, life insurance is viewed as a mere wagering contract entered into for profit.

    b. A life insurance policy that lacks the requisite insurable interest at the time of policy inception is a wagering contract and hence illegal. However, if the parties decide to observe the promises made under the contract, the death proceeds will be viewed as profits subject to income taxation.

    c. The requirement of insurable interest generally applies only at the time of policy inception. Therefore, assuming insurable interest exists when a policy is issued, the fact that it does not exist when the policy matures as a death claim will not subject the proceeds to income taxation. The tax-free nature of the death proceeds will be preserved under these circumstances.

14. When the death proceeds of a life insurance policy owned by a corporation to fund a buy-sell agreement are paid directly to shareholders as beneficiaries, the proceeds are taxable as dividends (because the result is the same as if the proceeds had been received tax free as life insurance proceeds by the corporation and then distributed to the shareholders as dividends).

15. Answers:

    a. If the corporation pays premiums on a life insurance policy where the shareholders are beneficiaries, the premiums will be taxable to the shareholders as dividends and nondeductible to the corporation.

    b. If the corporation pays premiums on a life insurance policy where the shareholders are beneficiaries as well as owners of the policy, the premiums will still be taxable to the shareholders as dividends and nondeductible to the corporation.

16. Answers:

    a. Premiums paid on life insurance owned by a qualified charitable organization are deductible to the donor as a charitable contribution, subject to the charitable contributions limitations.

    b. The Code denies a charitable deduction for gifts to charities where less than the taxpayer's entire interest in the property is contributed.

17. The requirements for premium payments to be deductible as alimony by the payer-spouse and taxable to the payee-spouse are that:

    • the payments be made in cash and terminate at the death of the payee-spouse

    • the payments be made under a divorce decree or separation agreement

    • the parties not be members of the same household and do not file joint tax returns

    • the payments not be for child support

    • the payments be made for at least 3 years unless either spouse dies or the payee-spouse remarries

18. Answers:

    a. Where an employee is the policyowner and the employer has no beneficial interest in the policy, premium payments by the employer on an individual policy insuring the life of the employee may be deductible by the employer as an ordinary and necessary business expense if they are considered reasonable additional compensation to the employee for services rendered.

    b. The premium payments by the employer are taxable compensation to the employee when paid.

19. The employee must generally include in gross income each year the value of the economic benefit received, which is measured by one of several different methods

prescribed by IRS Regs 1.61–22 and 1.7872–15. These methods calculate the taxable benefit based upon the employee's age and the amount of insurance protection.

20. Answers:

    a. This provision is the most significant exception to the general rule that interest deductions on policy loans are disallowed. The key person rule provides that interest on loan amounts not in excess of $50,000 per insured person is deductible if the insured is a "key person." The total number of key persons per business taxpayer may not exceed the GREATER of:

        - five individuals or
        - the LESSER of

            – 5 percent of the total number of officers and employees of the business taxpayer, or
            – 20 individuals

        This restriction means that in order for a business taxpayer to have more than five key persons for purposes of the tax rules for interest deductions on policy loans, the taxpayer has to have more than 100 employees. In addition, in order to have the maximum number of 20 key persons, the business taxpayer claiming the interest deductions would have to have at least 400 employees.

    b. If an insurance contract was entered into before June 21, 1986, the key person rules and the $50,000 of indebtedness limitation do not apply. Interest on loans connected with such contracts may be deductible, subject to other layers of rules imposed by IRC Sec. 264.

21. Husky will be able to deduct interest payments because the loan qualifies under the "key person" rule. However, the amount of interest deductible may be limited by the Moody's rate, depending upon the rate of interest specified in the policy.

22. If the indebtedness is incurred or continued to purchase or carry a single premium life insurance contract, no interest deduction for policy loans is allowable even if the interest qualifies under any other rules. A "single premium contract" is one in which substantially all the premiums are paid within a 4-year period from the date of purchase, or a contract for which an amount is deposited with the insurer for payment of a substantial number of future premiums on the contract.

# Self-Test Answers for Chapter 16

1. False. Death benefits payable under an annuity contract do not qualify for the exclusion applicable to life insurance proceeds.

2. False. Lump-sum proceeds payable by reason of the insured's death are generally excluded from the gross income of individuals, trusts, and estates.

3. False. If the amount is received with respect to a death occurring on or before October 22, 1986, a surviving spouse is entitled to the $1,000 income exclusion for payments received under all options except the interest-only option. With respect to insureds whose death occurred after October 22, 1986, the $1,000 interest exclusion was repealed.

4. True.

5. True.

6. True.

7. True.

8. True.

9. False. The contingent beneficiary will be taxed in the same manner as the primary beneficiary. The contingent beneficiary may exclude the same portion of each installment from his or her gross income as the primary beneficiary was entitled to exclude.

10. True.

11. False. The transfer-for-value rule applies to the transfer of a life insurance policy for valuable consideration. When the insured dies, the transferee will have taxable income on that portion of death proceeds in excess of the amount of consideration paid on the transfer, plus the total net premiums subsequently paid by the transferee.

12. False. A transfer to another shareholder is not an exception to the transfer-for-value rule.

13. True.

14. True.

15. True.

16. True.

17. False. The covered employee must generally include in gross income each year the value of the "economic benefit" received as determined by IRS guidance on this subject.

18. False. IRC Sec. 264 prohibits a deduction by any taxpayer for premiums paid on life insurance contracts if the taxpayer is directly or indirectly a beneficiary.

19. True.

20. True.

21. False. Interest on loans from single-premium life insurance policies cannot be deducted.

# Chapter 17

## Answers to Review Questions

1. Policy loans and partial withdrawals of funds from modified endowment contracts (MECs) are subject to last-in first-out (LIFO) treatment to determine the applicable taxes. This means that any income earned on the contract fund is taxed as if it was withdrawn before the policyowner's cost basis in the contract. In addition to the regular income tax, a 10 percent penalty tax is generally applicable to taxable gains withdrawn from a MEC before the policyowner reaches age 59 1/2. However, the 10 percent penalty does not apply to payments attributable to disability or to annuitized payments.

2. Answers:

   a. no
   b. yes
   c. no
   d. yes
   e. no

3. A "material change" results in the application of the 7-pay test to a policy as of the date of the material change. If the policy fails the 7-pay test, it will then be treated as a MEC. Note that a material change does not automatically cause the policy to be treated as a MEC. A policy that experiences a change will not be a MEC if it then passes the 7-pay test.

4. Answers:

   a. If there is a reduction of policy death benefits during the first 7 policy years, the 7-pay test will be applicable to the policy after the reduction. The test will be applied as if the contract had originally been issued at the reduced benefit level.
   b. With respect to policies entered into or materially changed on or after September 14, 1989, that insure more than one life (so-called survivorship policies), a reduction in death benefits *after* the first 7 contract years will also cause the policy to be subject to the 7-pay test as if the policy had originally been issued at the reduced benefit level.

# Self-Test Answers for Chapter 17

1. False. The 10 percent penalty will apply only to that portion of a withdrawal from a MEC that is subject to the federal income tax; that is, the portion attributable to the gain in the policy on a LIFO basis. In addition, the penalty tax is generally applicable to gains withdrawn from a MEC before the policyowner reaches age 59½. Moreover, it does not apply to payments attributable to disability or annuitized payments.

2. True.

3. True.

# Chapter 18

## Answers to Review Questions

1.  There are four legal characteristics that traditionally distinguish a corporation from other forms of business operation. These characteristics are:

    *   limited liability
    *   transferability of interest
    *   centralized management
    *   continuity of life

2.  An organization formed as a corporation under state law will generally be taxed as a corporation under federal law.

3.  The basic tax disadvantage is the potential of double taxation of earnings. The non-tax disadvantages include the fact that the corporate form lends itself to control of the minority by the majority and that corporate form has to be strictly observed; this entails charter documents, bylaws, and board of directors' as well as shareholders' meetings.

4.  The non-tax advantages of corporate status are the ability to freely transfer ownership and the limited liability of the owners. One of the tax advantages of corporate status is that the overall tax result may be lower federal income taxes if the corporation does not pay out substantial dividends. Although dividends remain preferentially taxed, they are still nondeductible by the corporation. The ability to time the receipt and taxation of income enables the owners to reduce their ultimate tax liability by allowing some income to remain in the corporation and be taxed at lower rates. In addition, employees of the corporation are entitled to receive a number of tax-free benefits that are tax deductible to the corporation, the major requirement being that these benefits must be reasonable in amount and provided in return for services rendered.

5.  In an S corporation, the firm's net income (i.e., ordinary income) is taxed directly to its shareholders. This enables shareholders of a small, closely held corporation to obtain the tax and non-tax advantages of corporate form without its disadvantages. The S corporation election avoids double taxation of corporate income upon the payment of dividends. This still exists even with lower dividend tax rates. It also avoids the problems of a penalty on accumulated earnings as well as the personal holding company tax. Depreciation as well as corporate income and losses will be immediately passed through to the shareholders.

    An S corporation election may also be indicated when shareholders intend to withdraw substantially all corporate earnings and (1) not all stockholders are employees who could justify their shares as salary payments, (2) the amount of earnings is so great that any attempt to pay them out as salaries would result in unreasonably high salaries, or (3) the corporation has taxable income that would be taxed at a corporate rate higher than the shareholders' individual marginal rates without an S election. The S election avoids the double tax that occurs to both a corporation and its shareholders when a dividend is paid out of earnings. Circumstances will dictate whether an S election will help in this regard.

    By an irrevocable and unqualified gift of shares of stock, a taxpayer can arrange to *split* income with another family member. Thus it is possible to transfer income to lower-bracket donees. By getting stock into the hands of various family members, it is possible to shift income to other taxpayers despite the fact that the income may be used to satisfy support or other family obligations that the donor would otherwise have to pay with after-tax dollars.

In fact, a taxpayer could even use the S corporation election to allow the corporation to continue income payments to the taxpayer at retirement (or to the taxpayer's spouse should the taxpayer predecease him or her) without double tax consequences.

6. Jones will be able to deduct the corporation's losses on his individual return if the corporation elects to be taxed as an S corporation.

7. To qualify for S corporation status, the following requirements must be met:

   - An S corporation can have only one class of stock.
   - An S corporation must have no more than 100 shareholders. Members of the same family are treated as one shareholder.
   - An S corporation can have no shareholder other than an individual, an estate, or certain types of trusts (except for qualified Subchapter S subsidiary corporations).
   - An S corporation must be a domestic corporation—that is, incorporated in the United States.
   - An S corporation may not have nonresident alien shareholders.

8. Answers:

   a. S corporation status can be terminated in any of the following ways:

      First, the corporation can elect to revoke the election with the consent of the shareholders who own more than 50 percent of the stock.

      Second, the election terminates if the corporation no longer qualifies as a "small business corporation"—that is, if it has more than 100 shareholders, or a nonresident alien acquires stock, or if an entity other than permitted shareholders acquires stock. Also the issuance of a second class of stock would terminate the election.

      Third, if more than 25 percent of the S corporation's gross receipts for 3 successive tax years is from certain types of passive income and the corporation has accumulated earnings and profits from its days prior to the S election, the election will be terminated. Certain banks and other companies are exempted from this rule.

   b. Voluntary revocations generally result in an inability to reelect the S status for 5 years without obtaining IRS consent to the reelection. The IRS can, in appropriate circumstances, waive the 5-year waiting period and permit the corporation to make a new election effective for the following taxable year. Also, if an S corporation election is invalid or late, the IRS may grant relief if the proper remedial action is taken by the corporation.

9. The general rule is that when property is exchanged for stock in a corporation, there is a *sale or exchange*. In the absence of any other provisions in the Code, there would be a recognized gain or loss. The amount of gain or loss is measured by the difference between the amount realized in the transaction (the value of stock received) and the adjusted basis (the cost) of the property transferred to the corporation.

10. There are three formal requirements that must be satisfied in order to avoid recognition of gain when property is transferred to a newly formed corporation.

    First, there must be one or more persons transferring property (which may include cash) to the newly formed corporation.

    Second, the transfer must be solely in exchange for stock in such a corporation.

    Third, the transferors (the person or persons transferring cash and/or property to the corporation in return for stock of the corporation) must be in control immediately after the exchange.

11. A transferor of appreciated property who receives stock in a corporation in exchange for the property and realizes a gain on the transfer generally does not recognize the gain if he or she is in control of the corporation immediately after the transfer. However, since Jules received cash (boot) in addition to stock, gain is recognized to the extent of the lesser of the cash received ($20,000) or the gain realized ($70,000). In this case, the gain recognized would be $20,000.

12. Answers:

    a. Upon the formation of a corporation, no gain or loss is generally recognized as long as the transfer of property to the corporation is solely in exchange for the corporation's own stock and the transferors are in control of the corporation (under IRC Sec. 351) immediately after the transfer. In the event that money or other property is received, gain will be recognized but losses will not. A stockholder's basis in the stock received from the corporation will be the same as the basis in the property contributed, but it will be decreased by any money the stockholder receives in the exchange and then increased by the amount of any gain the stockholder must recognize. When applying these general rules to the five stockholders, the following will result:

        A has no realized gain, so there could not be any recognized gain. His basis in the X stock is his basis in the cash $50.

        B has a realized gain of $50, but has no recognized gain since her transfer qualifies under the general rule of nonrecognition. Her basis in the X stock is the same as her basis in the contributed property $50.

        C has a realized gain of $10, but it has no recognized gain since its transfer qualifies under the general rule of nonrecognition. Its basis in the X stock is its basis in the contributed property $10.

        D has a realized gain of $20 and a recognized gain of $10 since he received boot. His basis in the X stock is his basis in the property contributed ($10), decreased by cash received ($10), and increased by gain recognized ($10). Therefore his basis is $10.

        E has a realized loss of $10, but it is not a recognized loss. His basis in the X stock is the basis of his contributed property ($30) minus the amount of money received ($10) for a basis of $20. It would be more advantageous to E to sell the property to the X Corporation, recognize his loss, and then invest $20 in cash in the corporation.

    b. X Corporation has no gain or loss upon the receipt of cash or property in exchange for its stock. Therefore X Corporation has no gain to recognize.

    c. X is not entitled to elect S corporation status because the election is limited to corporations whose shareholders are individuals, estates, and certain types of grantor or voting trusts. C, one of the shareholders of X Corporation, is a corporation itself.

13. The costs of creating a corporation ordinarily constitute capital expenditures. However, most of those costs may be amortized (that is, deducted by the corporation) in even amounts over a period of 180 months beginning with the month the corporation begins business. Subject to restrictions, $5,000 of such costs can be deducted in the corporation's first year of business.

14. Bonds are a favored means of raising corporate capital. One reason for this is that a corporation will obtain a deduction for the interest paid on the indebtedness. By contrast, no deduction is allowed for dividends paid on either preferred or common stock. As long as a corporation can earn money at a higher rate (with the cash raised by issuing the

bond) than it costs the corporation (in interest necessary to service the debt), it usually makes sense for the corporation to borrow money. This is known as "leverage."

Another reason bonds are favored over stock is that the accumulation of earnings and profits within the corporation to pay debt obligations can be justified more readily than accumulating earnings to redeem stock. This helps avoid an additional tax on an unreasonable accumulation of earnings.

15. Answers:

    a. Questions asked by the court to ascertain whether or not Rollo Corporation is thinly capitalized would include:

- Was there an intention by shareholders to enforce payment of the debt?
- Was there collateral for the debt?
- Was there a debt instrument (note), and did it give the shareholders management or voting rights (like stock)?
- What was the ratio of debt to equity?

       Basically, the court would examine all the factors relevant to determine if a "loan" by shareholders was in reality more like an ownership interest (stock) than a debtor-creditor relationship.

    b. If the amount of debt exceeds shareholders' equity by more than four to one, the corporation may be thinly capitalized.

16. Answers:

    a. The rates are 15 percent of the first $50,000 of taxable income, 25 percent of the next $25,000, 34 percent on amounts of taxable income between $75,001 and $100,000, 39 percent on amounts between $100,001 and $335,000, 34 percent on amounts between $335,001 and $10 million, 35 percent on amounts over $10 million up to $15 million, 38 percent on amounts over $15 million up to $18,333,333, and 35 percent on amounts over $18,333,333.

    b. The taxable income of a "qualified personal service corporation" is taxed at a flat rate of 35 percent.

17. The steps in computing corporate taxable income are:

$$\begin{array}{ll} & \text{Gross Income} \\ \text{Minus:} & \text{Ordinary Deductions} \\ \text{Minus:} & \text{Special Deductions} \\ & \text{Taxable Income} \end{array}$$

Corporate gross income includes such items as profit from sales and receipts from services. Subtracted from gross income are ordinary deductions and special deductions. Ordinary deductions include such items as compensation of officers and salary, charitable contributions, repair expenses, interest paid on indebtedness, deductions for depreciation, advertising, and corporate contributions to pension and profit-sharing plans. In addition, a corporation would also receive a carryover deduction for a net operating loss. Special deductions include such items as the dividends-received deduction. Taxable income is what is left after taking ordinary and special deductions. It is also the amount to which the corporate income tax rates are applied.

18. Answers:

    a. Reasonableness is a question of determining the amount that would ordinarily be paid for similar services by corporations under similar circumstances.

b. Only compensation paid by a publicly held corporation can be classified as "excessive employee remuneration." If the compensation paid to the executive is over $1 million per year, it typically would be considered "excessive" and not deductible by the corporation. Compensation for purposes of the definition of "excessive employee remuneration" does not include commissions, contributions to qualified plans, and tax-free fringe benefits. It also does not include any compensation that is "performance based." The $1 million limitation applies only to the CEO of the company and its four most highly compensated officers. Therefore it will apply only to a maximum of five employees in any given corporation.

19. Qualified production activities include the manufacture or development of tangible personal property; most computer or video game software; certain film productions; electricity, water, and natural gas production; and construction or substantial renovation of real property. The performance of engineering or architectural services also generally qualifies.

20. Answers:

a. The maximum amount a corporation may deduct as a charitable contribution in a given taxable year is 10 percent of its taxable income. This requires that certain adjustments be made to taxable income before the maximum deduction is computed.

b. If a corporation should make a contribution in excess of 10 percent of its adjusted taxable income, it can carry the excess forward for up to 5 years and apply it as a deduction to reduce its future taxable income.

21. Secane is able to carry back its net operating loss to the 2 previous years and carry it forward for 20 subsequent years. Secane may elect to utilize only the carryforward period.

22. A corporation cannot offset capital losses against ordinary income. It may only use capital losses as an offset against capital gains. In doing so, a corporation is permitted to carry an unused net capital loss back 3 years and then, if further loss still remains, carry the excess over to the 5 succeeding years.

23. Answers:

a. Daffy Defense Corporation is entitled to deduct amounts paid for salaries as long as they are reasonable. What is reasonable is determined by the facts in each case. An amount that would ordinarily be paid for like services by like business firms under similar circumstances would be reasonable.

b. Daffy Defense Corporation cannot deduct its capital loss currently because a corporation can only deduct its capital losses to the extent of its capital gains. Daffy Defense has no capital gains this year. However, the capital loss can be carried back for 3 years and then, if not used up, forward for 5 years.

c. Daffy Defense Corporation can deduct the full amount of its charitable contribution this year since it will almost certainly be less than 10 percent of its taxable income.

24. A corporation is allowed a special deduction for a percentage of dividends received during its tax year from stock it holds in certain other corporations. To be eligible for the deduction, these dividends must be distributions from the earnings and profits of taxable domestic corporations.

The amount of the dividends-received deduction can vary depending on how much stock in the paying corporation is owned by the receiving corporation. The dividends-received deduction is 70 percent if the receiving corporation owns less than 20 percent of the paying corporation. If the receiving corporation owns 20 percent or more but less than 80 percent of the paying corporation, the dividends-received deduction is 80 percent. Different rules apply if the corporation receiving the dividends owns 80 percent or more of the corporation paying the dividends. If certain conditions are met, the dividends-received deduction is 100 percent.

25. The accumulated-earnings tax is a tax imposed on every corporation that is formed or used for the purpose of avoiding personal income tax with respect to its shareholders by permitting earnings and profits to accumulate instead of being distributed. The purpose of the tax is to discourage the use of a corporation as an accumulation vehicle to shelter its individual stockholders from taxation resulting from dividend distributions. Accumulations of $250,000 or less will automatically be considered to be for the reasonable needs of the business. Accumulations of $150,000 or less will be considered to be for the reasonable needs of the business in the case of professional service corporations.

    The penalty for accumulating earnings beyond the reasonable needs of the business is taxation at a rate of 20 percent. This penalty tax is payable in addition to the regular tax payable by the firm. If applicable, the tax is imposed only on accumulated taxable income, an amount derived from the taxable income of the corporation for the particular year in question. Thus the tax does not apply to all the accumulated earnings and profits of the corporation but only to the accumulated taxable income of the year or years in which the tax is asserted.

26. The accumulated-earnings tax is imposed if earnings and profits accumulate beyond the reasonable needs of the business. What constitutes the reasonable needs of the business is a factual determination in each case.

    a. Here, where Zoom Corporation accumulates earnings and profits so that its shareholders can avoid taxation at higher rates, the prohibitive purpose is present. Therefore, the accumulated-earnings tax would be imposed on all accumulated taxable income in excess of the accumulated-earnings credit.
    b. On the other hand, an accumulation in the form of cash values on key person policies is a reasonable need as long as the policies were purchased for a valid business purpose of the corporation.

27. The purchase of $500,000 of key person life insurance by the Price Corporation as well as the earnings used to pay policy premiums will not, per se, subject the corporation to the accumulated-earnings penalty tax if it is not accumulating earnings beyond the reasonable needs of the business. Generally, hedging against the loss of a key employee's service because of unexpected death is considered to be a reasonable business need.

    Most corporations will have little trouble in proving a reasonable business need for most of the earnings they retain. However, corporations that never pay dividends, like the Price Corporation, are generally suspect and must be prepared to prove with appropriate records that they have specific plans to use the accumulated earnings.

    In determining whether or not Price Corporation's accumulated taxable income for the current year is being retained for the reasonable needs of the business, the availability of prior years' accumulated earnings must also be considered. Since Price Corporation's past years' accumulations are more than sufficient to meet current needs or anticipated growth, it would have no justification for accumulating this year's earnings whether to purchase key person life insurance or for use to cover some other business need. Therefore, to avoid aggravating Price Corporation's potential accumulated-earning tax problem, it should allocate some of the prior years' accumulated earning to purchase key person cash value life insurance while also instituting a dividend program. The purchase of key person cash value life insurance with prior years' accumulated earnings will help to alleviate Price Corporation's potential problem, even though it can accumulate a surplus of up to $250,000 of earnings and profits without any possibility of being subject to the tax.

28. Answers:

    a.  Personal holding companies are subject to taxation in addition to the regular corporate taxes. The additional tax is currently imposed at a rate of 20 percent. It applies to undistributed personal holding company income, which is basically taxable income minus taxes paid and dividends distributed.

    b.  The principal way to avoid the penalty tax is to cause the corporation to distribute dividends. If liability for personal-holding-company tax is found, the Code allows a corporation to mitigate this tax liability by paying a retroactive deficiency dividend.

29. The rule is that when appreciated property is distributed in any type of distribution by a corporation, it must recognize gain (but not loss). This rule is applicable to distributions of dividends and in redemption of stock. The amount realized would be equal to the gain that would have been realized if the property had been sold at the time of the distribution. Gain is measured by the extent to which the property's fair market value exceeds its adjusted basis.

# Self-Test Answers for Chapter 18

1. True.
2. False. Limited liability means that a creditor of a corporation cannot proceed against the individual shareholders personally to satisfy a corporate debt.
3. True.
4. True.
5. True.
6. True.
7. True.
8. False. An S corporation may have up to 100 shareholders.
9. True.
10. False. On the contrary, there are many instances under the Internal Revenue Code where property of an existing business may be transferred to a newly formed corporation solely in exchange for the corporation's stock without recognition of gain.
11. True.
12. True.
13. False. A maximum of $5,000 of these expenses is deductible in the corporation's first year. The balance must be amortized over a 180-month period beginning with the month in which the corporation begins business.
14. True.
15. False. Corporate taxable income over $100,000 up to and $335,000 is taxed at 39 percent. This is currently the highest corporate rate.
16. False. The reasonableness test involves the determination of a salary that would ordinarily be paid for similar services by similar corporations under like circumstances.
17. False. If the compensation is excessive, it will be held to be "unreasonable" by the IRS regardless of whether the salary is specified in a salary agreement. The portion of the salary considered unreasonable is usually reclassified as a disguised dividend if the employee is a shareholder. Any amount recharacterized as a disguised dividend to a shareholder will not be deductible by the corporation. Also, any amount classified as "excessive employee remuneration" will not be deductible by the corporation.
18. True.
19. False. A corporation may deduct amounts up to 10 percent of its taxable income for contributions to qualified charities.
20. False. Corporations are not entitled to a net long-term capital-gain exclusion.
21. False. Generally, a corporation may deduct 70 percent of any dividends received from domestic corporations. The deduction may be 80 percent, or even 100 percent, of dividends received in some cases.
22. False. The accumulation of cash to purchase key person life insurance is considered a reasonable business need. Upon the death of a key employee, a corporation may require additional capital to replace the value of the employee's services. Therefore accumulations for this purpose would not be subject to the accumulated-earnings tax.
23. False. The personal-holding-company tax is currently imposed at a rate of 20 percent.
24. True.

# Chapter 19

## Answers to Review Questions

1. The maximum tax rate currently applicable to qualified dividends is 20 percent. These rates are equivalent to the rates currently applicable to most long-term capital gains of individuals. For lower-bracketed taxpayers, the rate of taxation on qualified dividends is either 15 or zero percent. These two lower rates apply to taxpayers whose incomes fall below $450,000 for joint filers and surviving spouses, $425,000 for heads of household, and $400,000 for single filers.

2. The general rule for taxing distributions of property from a corporation to its shareholders is that it will be taxed as a dividend to the extent of the corporation's current and accumulated earnings and profits.

3. Yes, the $200,000 distribution by Jimbo Corporation to its shareholders will be taxed to the shareholders as a dividend. Although Jimbo Corporation has no current earnings and profits, it had accumulated $400,000 of earnings and profits from prior years. Any portion of a distribution from that source will be treated as a dividend.

4. If there were neither current nor accumulated earnings and profits, the $200,000 distribution by Jimbo Corporation to its shareholders would not be treated as a dividend. The distribution would be treated as a nontaxable return of capital to the extent of the shareholders' basis in the stock. If any portion of the distribution exceeded the shareholders' basis in the stock, it would be taxed as a capital gain.

5. Answers:

    a. The first $100,000 will be taxed to Zsa Zsa as a dividend since there are accumulated earnings and profits.
    b. The next $30,000 reduces the basis of Zsa Zsa's interest in her stock to zero.
    c. The remaining $20,000 will be taxed to Zsa Zsa as capital gain.

6. Transactions that could be treated as so-called "constructive dividends" include the following:

    - where a debtor of the corporation makes payments directly to the corporation's shareholders rather than to the corporation itself
    - where a corporation relieves a shareholder of liability for a debt the shareholder owes the corporation
    - where a corporation receives life insurance proceeds and then later pays the amount of the proceeds to its shareholders on a pro rata basis
    - where a corporation pays premiums on a life insurance policy that is owned by and insures its principal shareholder, and the corporation is not the beneficiary of the policy
    - where a corporation sells property to its shareholders for less than the property's fair market value (a "bargain sale")
    - where a shareholder-employee of a corporation is paid a salary that is more than the value of the services furnished to the corporation
    - where a shareholder enjoys personal use of property owned by the corporation, such as a residence or a vehicle

        The IRS will examine the actual economic effect of such transactions in determining whether dividend tax treatment should be applied.

7. Answers:

a. The general rule provides that dividend treatment is applied to distributions to shareholders, including the proceeds of a redemption, to the extent of the corporation's current and accumulated earnings and profits.

b. Exceptions to the general rule apply to certain types of redemptions in which the redeemed shareholder's percentage of ownership in the corporation is materially affected by the redemption. If a given redemption qualifies under one of these exceptions, the transaction will be treated as a capital transaction for tax purposes. Sec. 302 allows such treatment for the following four types of redemptions:

- a redemption that is "not essentially equivalent to a dividend"
- a "substantially disproportionate" redemption
- a "complete" redemption
- a distribution to a noncorporate shareholder in "partial liquidation" of the distributing corporation

8. Answers:

    a.

(1) After the redemption, Frank still controls 100 percent of Hotdog Corporation.

(2) After the redemption, Frank has the same rights to Hotdog Corporation's profits as before the redemption.

(3) After the redemption, Frank's proportionate share of and claim on the assets of the Hotdog Corporation upon liquidation are the same as before the redemption.

    b. Yes. In all three instances Frank has gone from 100 percent to 50 percent. In other words, if Frank sold 50 shares to a friend, Frank's control of Hotdog, his rights to Hotdog's profits, and his proportionate share of and claim on Hotdog's assets would all now be 50 percent instead of 100 percent.

9. In order for a stock redemption to be considered "not essentially equivalent to a dividend," there must be a meaningful reduction in the shareholder's interest in the corporation. This is not a mathematical test, but a subjective one. Each redemption that a shareholder claims is "not essentially equivalent to a dividend" must be evaluated according to its particular facts.

10. In order for a redemption to be considered substantially disproportionate, it must meet the following requirements:

- After the redemption, the shareholder must own less than 50 percent of the total voting power of the corporation.
- The shareholder's percentage ownership of *voting* stock of the corporation after the redemption must be less than 80 percent of his or her percentage ownership of voting stock before the redemption.
- The shareholder's percentage ownership of *common* stock of the corporation after the redemption must also be less than 80 percent of his or her percentage ownership of common stock before the redemption.

11. The redemption qualifies as a substantially disproportionate redemption. Before the redemption Abigail owns 50/100, or 50 percent of the stock. After the redemption Abigail owns 25/75, or 33 percent of the stock. Note that Abigail meets the two qualifications—(1) her postredemption ownership ratio of 33 percent is less than 80 percent of her preredemption ratio, since 50 percent × 80 percent is 40 percent, and (2) after the redemption Abigail owns less than 50 percent of the voting and common shares.

12. Answers:

    a. This transaction is not a redemption. Anna is purchasing shares directly from Boyd. A redemption involves a corporation's purchase of its own stock.

    b. This transaction cannot qualify as a complete termination because Anna still owns stock after the redemption. It will also not qualify as a substantially disproportionate redemption. Before the redemption Anna owns 50/100, or 50 percent of the stock of the corporation. Afterward she owns 40/90, or 44 percent. Note that her postredemption percentage interest of 44 percent is not less than 80 percent of her preredemption percentage interest since 50 percent × 80 percent is 40 percent. The other test—that Anna must own less than 50 percent of the voting and common shares after the redemption—is met.

13. The rationale for attribution of ownership is that a shareholder may effectively control the operation of a corporation through shares owned by related individuals and entities as well as through shares he or she actually owns.

14. Answers:

    a. Nancy will be considered to own stock in Jordano that is owned by her mother.

    b. Nancy will not be considered to own stock in Jordano that is owned by her sister.

    c. Nancy will not be considered to own stock in Jordano that is owned by her grandmother.

    d. Nancy will be considered to own stock in Jordano that is owned by her son.

15. In the case of attribution to a shareholder from an entity, the general rule is that the shareholder will be considered to own stock owned by the entity in proportion to the shareholder's interest in the entity. Some situations involve modifications to this general rule.

16. In the case of attribution from an individual to an entity, the general rule is that the entity will be considered to own all the stock owned by the individual having an interest in the entity. There are modifications to this general rule that apply to trusts and to corporations.

17. To qualify for a waiver of family attribution in a complete redemption, a shareholder must comply with the following requirements:

- The redeemed shareholder may retain no interest in the corporation after the redemption. For these purposes "interest" includes the status of officer, director, or employee of the corporation. It is permissible for the redeemed shareholder to remain a creditor of the corporation.

- The redeemed shareholder must not acquire any prohibited interest in the corporation for a period of 10 years beginning on the date of the distribution of the redemption proceeds. However, if the redeemed shareholder receives stock in the corporation by bequest or inheritance, this provision is not violated.

- The redeemed shareholder must file an agreement with the IRS to notify it if any acquisition of a prohibited interest takes place within the 10-year period.

- The redeemed shareholder must not have acquired any portion of the stock redeemed during a 10-year period prior to the date of the redemption from a person whose stock would be attributable to the redeemed shareholder.

- The redeemed shareholder must not have transferred any stock in the redeeming corporation to any person whose stock would be attributed to the redeemed shareholder within a 10-year period before the date of distribution of the redemption proceeds. This requirement will not apply if the corporation also redeems such stock of the person to whom it was transferred by the redeemed shareholder.

18. Sec. 303 of the Code is a relief provision that applies to estates in which stock of a closely held corporation constitutes a substantial portion of total estate assets. The purpose of Sec. 303 is to provide liquidity for such estates in order to avoid forced sales of the closely held stock to meet tax obligations and administrative expenses. It allows distributions in redemption of such stock to be treated as made in exchange for a capital asset and therefore eligible for capital-gains treatment.

 To be eligible for a Sec. 303 redemption, the value of the stock in the redeeming corporation that is includible in the gross estate for federal estate tax purposes must be more than 35 percent of the value of the adjusted gross estate. The redemption proceeds eligible for favorable tax treatment are limited to the sum of the estate, inheritance, legacy, and succession taxes for which the estate is liable and the amount of funeral and administration expenses allowable as deductions to the estate. Only that portion of taxes and expenses that the redeemed shareholder is legally obligated to pay is considered in determining the amount of proceeds allowable.

19. Sec. 303 guarantees sale or exchange treatment to the extent of death taxes, funeral costs, and administrative costs if (a) the stock of the redeeming corporation is includible in the decedent's gross estate and (b) the value of the stock is more than 35 percent of the decedent's adjusted gross estate and the distribution occurs within the same time period as the time for payment of estate tax, including any extensions. If the conditions of Sec. 303 are met, it overrides those sections of the Code otherwise applicable, including the attribution rules.

20. A corporation will generally redeem the stock of a decedent shareholder at a price equal to the stock's current fair market value. For income tax purposes an estate or its beneficiary receives a "stepped-up" basis in a decedent's assets that is generally equal to the value of the assets as of the date of the decedent's death. Therefore if a redemption is made under Sec. 303 within a short time after the decedent's death, the redemption price should be equal to or very close to the basis in the stock held by the estate or the beneficiary.

21. The Code states specifically that corporate accumulations may be made to fund a Sec. 303 redemption without being subject to the accumulated-earnings tax. However, such accumulations are specifically exempt only when made in the corporation's taxable year in which the decedent died or any taxable year thereafter. Therefore accumulations prior to the year of the decedent's death to meet an anticipated funding need for a redemption may present the corporation with an accumulated-earnings tax problem.

 If the IRS can show that the funding objective was not for a corporate purpose, but only for the benefit of the shareholder or the shareholder's estate, the accumulated-earnings tax may become a problem. It may be difficult to convince the IRS that a Sec. 303 redemption serves a business purpose of the corporation.

# Self-Test Answers for Chapter 19

1. True.
2. False. A dividend does not include a return of capital. It is a taxable distribution to the extent of the corporation's current and accumulated earnings and profits.
3. True.
4. False. "Qualified" dividends are currently taxed to individual taxpayers at a maximum rate of 20 percent (zero percent and 15 percent for lower-bracket taxpayers).
5. False. A distribution by a corporation that has no current or accumulated earnings and profits cannot be taxable as a dividend.
6. False. When a corporation with no accumulated or current earnings and profits makes a distribution to its stockholders, the distribution is first applied to reduce the basis of the stock to zero. Any excess is taxed as a capital gain.
7. True.
8. False. Redemptions taxed as capital transactions involve situations in which the percentage of ownership is materially affected.
9. True.
10. True.
11. True.
12. True.
13. False. The postredemption ratio under the 80 percent test must reflect the reduction in the total number of shares outstanding.
14. True.
15. False. If a corporation redeems all the stock of a shareholder in a redemption that completely terminates the shareholder's interest in the corporation and the shareholder's family does not own stock in the same corporation, the redemption will be taxed as a sale or exchange.
16. True.
17. False. The attribution rules apply to stock owned directly or indirectly by or for a partnership or estate. The stock is generally considered as owned proportionately by the entity's partners or beneficiaries.
18. True.
19. False. A Sec. 303 redemption to pay death taxes will be allowed if the value of the redeeming corporation's stock included in the gross estate exceeds 35 percent of the adjusted gross estate.
20. False. A Sec. 303 redemption is allowed to the extent the redemption proceeds do not exceed the total of all federal and state death taxes (including interest, if any) and funeral costs and administration expenses allowed as deductions to the estate.

# Chapter 20

## Answers to Review Questions

1. Under state law, business organizations may be formed as corporations, general partnerships, limited partnerships, limited liability partnerships, limited liability companies, or as variations of these business forms. However, all of these various types of entities are classified as either partnerships or corporations for federal tax purposes.

   With the development of these "hybrid" business entities, it became administratively difficult for the IRS to classify them for tax purposes based upon the presence or absence of a preponderance of corporate characteristics. As a result, a more flexible system of classification (often referred to as "check the box") was developed.

   Under this approach, organizations that are not incorporated under state law will generally be permitted to choose whether to be taxed as corporations or partnerships. In most cases, they will choose to be taxed as partnerships.

2. Both limited liability companies and limited liability partnerships are unincorporated under state law but exhibit at least one corporate characteristic—limited liability.

3. It is important that a particular organization be taxed as the parties involved intended because of the tax distinctions between a corporation and a partnership. When an organization is treated for tax purposes as a partnership, the profits earned by the partners will be taxed only once on their individual returns. When profits are earned by a corporation, they are taxed once to the business and then taxed again to the shareholders if they are paid out in the form of dividends. Also, if a business is classified as a partnership, the partners may deduct their share of any net losses on their individual returns. If the business is a corporation, losses may be claimed only by the corporation and are not available to offset the shareholder's other income. Therefore it may be important to characterize an organization as a partnership if certain potential tax pitfalls are to be avoided.

4. According to the aggregate theory, a partnership is considered as an aggregate of individual co-owners who have bound themselves together with the intention of sharing gains and losses. The partnership itself has no existence separate and apart from its members. To the extent this theory influences tax law, a partnership is nothing more than the sum of its individual members. Tax liability passes through the partnership directly to each partner, who pays tax on his or her share of the profits just as though he or she realized the share of income as an individual.

   While the aggregate theory makes the partnership a conduit for some purposes, the entity theory recognizes that for certain other purposes the partnership is a separate entity that is distinct from its members. Accordingly, the partnership must file an income tax return for information-purposes only. The return provides a way to inform both the IRS and the individual partners how the profits and losses are allocated. Three other indicia of the entity theory are that a partnership has a taxable year, its own accounting method, and the right to exercise various income tax elections. Also in support of the entity theory is the fact that partners who engage in transactions with their own partnerships are typically treated taxwise like a stranger. In other words, when a partner is not acting in his or her capacity as a partner, a transaction between that partner and the partnership is treated as if it was conducted between the partnership and an unrelated third person.

5. The general rule is that the basis a contributing partner has in property he or she contributes to the partnership becomes his or her initial basis for his or her partnership interest. Stated more precisely, the amount of cash an individual contributes plus the

adjusted basis in property the individual contributes becomes the original basis in the individual's new partnership interest.

6. Answers:

    a. The form of business for tax purposes of Bedford Falls Auto Repairs is a partnership. Bert and Ernie have the objective of carrying on a business and sharing profits and losses equally. There is no limited liability as long as Bert and Ernie do not incorporate. There is no centralization of management because each partner may act on behalf of the partnership in his capacity as a partner.

       The form of the business has a strong effect on the tax liability of Bert and Ernie. If Bedford Falls Auto Repairs is taxed as a corporation, then Bert and Ernie are only taxed on their compensation and dividends from the business. The corporation must pay tax on its own taxable income. If Bedford Falls is taxed as a partnership, then each partner pays tax on his share of the partnership's income. The partnership itself pays no income tax.

    b. Bert and Ernie have no gain to recognize upon the formation of the partnership due to the nonrecognition provisions in the Code.

    c. A partner's basis in his or her partnership interest is the basis in the property he or she contributed to the partnership, reduced by liabilities assumed by the partnership and increased by liabilities assumed by the partner. Applying this general rule, Bert's basis is $33,000 plus $6,000 in liabilities assumed (1/2 of $12,000), for a total basis of $39,000. Ernie's basis is $22,000 reduced by $6,000 for liabilities relieved, or a total basis of $16,000. Note that the basis is not the same as the amount of capital contribution. Each partner has contributed equity of $33,000.

7. When contributed property is subject to indebtedness, the original basis of the contributor's partnership interest must be lowered by the portion of the indebtedness taken over by the other partners.

8. A partnership must file a federal income tax return (IRS Form 1065) that is for informational purposes only. A civil penalty is now imposed on any partnership that fails to file a complete partnership information return, unless reasonable cause is shown. This penalty is in addition to criminal penalties for willful failure to file a return, supply information, or pay tax.

9. The partners must include in their individual tax returns their distributive shares of the partnership income or loss. They must also take into account (and report on their 1040s) a number of separate partnership items, including:

    • capital gains and losses
    • Sec. 1231 gains and losses
    • charitable contributions
    • dividends received by the partnership from stockholdings

       The partners would then add their share of each of the above items to their individual income and deductions.

       In addition, a partner can obtain a salary or guaranteed payment. A guaranteed payment is a sum paid to a partner, regardless of whether the partnership has income. Such a payment is ordinary income to the recipient partner.

10. If only services are contributed, and the contributing partner receives an interest in partnership capital (that is, an interest in the property contributed by his or her copartners), then the contributing partner realizes current ordinary income as long as there are no

substantial restrictions on that partner's right to withdraw or dispose of his or her interest in partnership capital. When such income is realized, that income will be added to the partner's basis.

11. Answers:

    a. The partnership will report the loss on the partnership informational return (Form 1065).

    b. Each partner reports his distributive share (in this case, 50 percent) of the losses on his individual income tax return to the extent that his basis in his partnership interest exceeds zero. Losses in excess of his basis may be carried over to future years when the partner's basis is greater than zero.

12. Generally speaking, the distributive shares of each item are to be determined in accordance with the partnership agreement. If the partnership does not cover a particular item, the partner's distributive share of that item is the same percentage as his or her percentage share of partnership income or loss.

13. Sometimes partners, through the partnership agreement, attempt to shift an item to the taxpayer in whose hands the item will be most beneficial. This allocation of one type of item to the partner who can obtain the greatest tax benefit (such as an allocation of all depreciation deductions to the highest tax bracket partner) may be ignored by the IRS. If such a provision does not have "substantial economic effect," the partners' shares of that item will be readjusted by the IRS just as if the partnership agreement contained no provision as to the item; that is, each partner's distributive share of that item is determined in accordance with his or her share of partnership income or loss.

14. Answers:

    a. The partnership must utilize the same tax year as that of its majority partner or principal partners unless there is a business purpose (such as a natural business cycle) for use of a fiscal year. In most cases this will be a calendar year. Therefore Wonder Burgers must file its informational return on April 15 of each year.

    b. Wonder Burgers has no tax to pay on amounts earned. The partners must include their proportionate share of the partnership's income in their individual gross income for the year.

15. Jessica's distributive share will be deemed the same as her share of profits and losses.

16. Answers:

    a. A partner's basis is increased by the following three factors:

        (1) his or her capital contributions

        (2) his or her distributive share of partnership income

        (3) his or her share of liabilities assumed

    b. A partner's basis is reduced by the following three factors:

        (1) his or her share of losses

        (2) his or her distributions or draws

        (3) his or her share of liabilities *relieved*

    c. Reasons for increases and reductions to a partner's basis are:

        • By increasing basis, the partner is being protected from having to pay tax on the additional capital invested in the partnership upon a subsequent disposition of his or her partnership interest.

- By reducing basis, the partner recognizes recoveries of capital invested in the partnership resulting from losses deducted against other income, distributions of property or money from the partnership to the partner, and decreases in the partner's share of partnership liabilities.

17. An individual partner's loss deduction cannot exceed his or her basis for the partnership interest at the end of the year for which the loss occurred. However, the partner is entitled to an unlimited carryover of nondeductible partnership losses.

18. A partner needs to know what his or her basis in his or her partnership interest is because basis is important in determining the amount of loss that can be recognized and deducted in any one tax year. It also affects taxation upon the disposition of a partnership interest on the partner's retirement or death.

19. Answers:

   a. John's distributive share of the loss is $15,000 since he and Bobby are equal partners (Bobby's share would also be $15,000).
   b. John may deduct $10,000 currently. His deduction is limited to his basis in the partnership. The remaining $5,000 loss may be carried over to future years.

20. Answers:

   a. The premiums paid by each partner are not tax deductible. However, on the death of a partner, the insurance proceeds received by each surviving partner are income tax free.
   b. The premiums paid by the partnership are not tax deductible. However, on the death of a partner, the insurance proceeds received by the partnership are income tax free.

21. John's gain will be taxed as capital gain with the exception of amounts attributable to unrealized receivables and inventory. These items will be treated as ordinary income.

22. Answers:

   a. Each partner's basis is determined each year by adding his capital contributions, his share of the partnership's income, and his share of any additional liabilities. His current basis is reduced by his share of losses, his distributions or draws, and his share of liabilities relieved.
   b. If Jim buys Don's partnership interest, Don's gain is treated as capital gain with the exception of amounts attributable to unrealized receivables and inventory, which will be treated as ordinary income. This partnership has unrealized receivables in the form of accounts receivable but has no inventory. Therefore Don's gain will be $50,000 of capital gain and $15,000 of ordinary income.
   c.

      (1) The $60,000 received for partnership property will not be taxed because Don's share of the partnership property, exclusive of unrealized receivables, is $60,000. If Don had received more than $60,000 for his partnership property, he would have a capital gain.

      (2) The amount received for unrealized receivables is treated as ordinary income. In this case Don has $15,000 of ordinary income.

      (3) The amount attributable to goodwill ($50,000) is treated as a capital gain to Don, since the partnership agreement states that payment will be made for goodwill. If the partnership agreement is silent as to goodwill, then any other payments made by a service partnership are treated as additional payments and are taxed as ordinary income to the retiring partner. If the

retiring partner has ordinary income, the partnership has a deduction for the same amount.

23. If a retiring partner's interest in a service partnership is liquidated, the following tax consequences result:

   a. Payments for partnership property (exclusive of unrealized receivables, inventory, and unspecified goodwill) that result in a gain to the taxpayer are treated as capital gain. Payments for unrealized receivables, inventory, and unspecified goodwill result in ordinary income.

   The remaining partners generally have the option to increase the basis of partnership assets in properties by the amount of gain recognized to the retiring partner. If the retiring partner receives ordinary income for inventory items, the partnership basis in those assets will also be increased. If the retiring partner receives ordinary income for unrealized receivables or unspecified goodwill, the remaining partners have a corresponding deduction from partnership income. If ABC were not a service partnership, it would not be entitled to a deduction for the unrealized receivables or unspecified goodwill.

   b. The retiring partner has ordinary income for amounts treated as additional payments that are part of his or her distributive share and not attributable to partnership property. Note that payment for goodwill can be treated as an additional payment (ordinary income) or partnership property (capital gain) depending upon whether the partnership agreement states that payment will be made for goodwill. If ABC were not a service partnership, any payment for goodwill would be taxed as capital gain.

   The partnership will obtain a deduction for additional payments taxed as ordinary income to the retiring partner.

24. In the case of a liquidation of a partnership interest other than that of a general partner in a service partnership, both unrealized receivables and goodwill are automatically treated as partnership property. As a result, the partnership in such cases receives no deduction for payments for such property. There is also no deduction to the partnership with respect to payments for inventory, although a basis adjustment is generally made corresponding to such payments.

   To the extent the partner receives more for his or her interest in the partnership's cash and other property than the partner's share of basis in those assets, he or she will have a capital gain. The remaining partners have the option of increasing the basis in partnership assets for the gain so recognized by the partner. However, any portion of the payments received for unrealized receivables and inventory that exceeds the partner's share of partnership basis in such assets is treated as ordinary income. The retiring partner must segregate the cash and other property from the inventory and unrealized receivables.

25. Basically, limited partnerships and their partners are taxed the same as general partnerships and their partners.

26. Answers:

   a. If there is economic (non-tax-motivated) reality to the arrangement, the partnership allocations of income will be accepted for income tax purposes.

   b. If the arrangement lacks economic reality, the IRS may ignore the entire partnership arrangement and reallocate income to properly reflect the interests of the partners.

27. Answers:

a. If a family member acquires a capital interest in a family partnership in which capital is a material income-producing factor, there are limitations on the amount that may be allocated as his or her distributive share of partnership income.

   First, the donor of the interest must be allocated an amount that represents reasonable compensation for services rendered to the partnership. The remaining income generally may be divided among the partners according to their agreement for sharing partnership profits and losses. However, that portion of the remaining income allocated to the donee may not be proportionately greater than that allocated to the donor on the basis of their respective capital interests.

   An interest purchased by one member of the family from another member of the family is considered to be created by gift for this purpose.

b. If a family member acquires an interest in a family partnership in which capital is not a material income-producing factor, the individual family member must contribute substantial or vital services; otherwise, his or her share of partnership income would be reallocated by the IRS to the other partners. Capital is not considered a material income-producing factor if the income of the business consists principally of fees, commissions, or other compensation for personal services performed by members or employees of the partnership.

# Self-Test Answers for Chapter 20

1.  True.
2.  True.
3.  False. The partnership itself is not a taxpayer. Therefore profits are taxed only once to each partner.
4.  True.
5.  True.
6.  False. No gain is recognized on the transfer of appreciated assets to a partnership. The contributor-partner will generally take as his or her original basis for his or her partnership interest the basis he or she had in the property contributed at the time of contribution.
7.  False. A partnership does file a partnership return, but only for informational purposes. A partnership does not pay income taxes.
8.  True.
9.  True.
10. False. When a partner lends money to his or her partnership as an outsider, his or her partnership basis is increased by his or her share of the partnership's liability to him or her.
11. True.
12. True.
13. True.
14. False. If the partnership agreement specifies that payments will be made for goodwill, the partners receiving liquidating distributions will report payments for goodwill as capital gain, but the payments are not deductible by the partnership. If the agreement is silent as to goodwill, the payments are taxable to the partners as ordinary income and are deductible by the partnership.
15. False. Payments to a retiring partner that are attributable to unrealized receivables are not deductible by a manufacturing partnership. Although the retiring partner will treat such amounts as ordinary income, the partnership treats such amounts as made-for-partnership property. No deduction is allowed.
16. True.
17. True.
18. True.
19. False. The donee must have dominion and control over the partnership interest in order to be taxed on his or her share of partnership income.
20. True.

# SAMPLE EXAMINATION—INCOME TAXATION

## NOTE

Below are 100 objective questions to be used as an additional review of material in *Fundamentals of Income Taxation*, 11th edition. The review will familiarize you with the format of American College objective examinations. These questions are followed by an Answer Key and an explanation of the answers.

## DIRECTIONS

Each of the questions or incomplete statements below is followed by four suggested answers or completions. Select the one that is best in each case and circle the letter that corresponding to that answer.

1.  Smith and Jones formed a partnership. Smith contributed a building with an original cost of $80,000, a fair market value of $100,000, and an adjusted basis of $40,000. Jones contributed $100,000 cash. Each partner is a material participant in partnership business. How much can Smith currently deduct if his share of the partnership's first-year operating loss is $45,000?

    (A) $5,000
    (B) $20,000
    (C) $40,000
    (D) $45,000

2.  Which of the following statements concerning the taxation of capital gains and losses of individual taxpayers is correct?

    (A) The maximum tax rate on long-term capital gains is generally 15 percent under current law.
    (B) Up to $3,000 of net capital losses ($1,500 if married filing separately) may be used to offset ordinary income in any given year.
    (C) "Collectibles" gain is taxed at regular ordinary income tax rates.
    (D) The portion of long-term gain attributable to unrecaptured depreciation is not taxable when real estate is sold.

3.  Michael and Mary, a married couple filing jointly, sell their home this year for $650,000. Their basis in the home, including cost and improvements, is $200,000. Mary purchased the home in her name many years ago and the couple has lived together there since that time. What amount of gain must Michael and Mary recognize from the sale?

    (A) $0
    (B) $200,000
    (C) $450,000
    (D) $650,000

4. Which of the following statements concerning the conventions used for calculating depreciation in the year an asset is placed in service is correct?

(A) Assets in the 5-year property class are subject to a "mid-month" convention.

(B) The convention for the year the property is placed in service does not apply in the year in which the property is disposed of.

(C) A "midquarter" convention applies if more than 40 percent of all property placed in service by a taxpayer during the year and otherwise qualifying for the "half-year" convention is placed in service during the last 3 months of the taxable year.

(D) Real estate is subject to a "half-year" convention.

5. Johnson makes a $500,000 building available five nights a week at no charge to the local Boy Scout Council. Which of the following statements correctly describes how the use of Johnson's property will be treated for purposes of the charitable contribution deduction?

(A) Johnson has a charitable deduction equal to the fair market value of the property.

(B) Johnson has no deduction for the rent-free occupancy.

(C) Johnson has a charitable deduction equal to the value of the rent-free occupancy but limited to 30 percent of his adjusted gross income.

(D) Johnson has a charitable deduction equal to the value of the rent-free occupancy but limited to 50 percent of his adjusted gross income.

6. Five years ago John purchased a portfolio of public-purpose municipal bonds for $85,000. During the current year he received $8,000 interest on these bonds. At the end of the current year he sold these bonds for $95,000. How much taxable income must John report for the current year as a consequence of owning and disposing of these bonds?

(A) $0

(B) $4,800

(C) $10,000

(D) $18,000

7. Which of the following statements concerning elements of personal income taxation is correct?

(A) The personal exemption amount is a fixed amount not indexed for inflation.

(B) The "kiddie tax" applies to the earned income of children under a specified age.

(C) Single taxpayers receive the highest standard deduction amount.

(D) The range of taxable income over which specific tax brackets will be applied depends on the filing status of the particular taxpayer(s).

8. Which of the following is an ordinary and necessary deductible business expense for Bob, a life insurance agent?

(A) the tuition fee for the two CLU courses he is taking toward his CLU designation

(B) the entire amount of his home telephone bill, since he often sets up appointments from home

(C) premiums for his homeowners' insurance

(D) the cost of commuting to his office

9. Which of the following statements concerning a taxpayer who wishes to contest a statutory notice of deficiency assessed against him is correct?

   (A) He may petition for a jury trial in the U.S. Court of Federal Claims without prepaying the deficiency.
   (B) He may petition the U.S. Tax Court to hear his case without prepaying the deficiency but is not entitled to a jury trial.
   (C) He may file a petition to have his case heard before a jury in the U.S. District Court without prepaying the deficiency.
   (D) He may petition for a jury trial in the U.S. Tax Court without prepaying the deficiency.

10. An employer maintains a group term life insurance plan for its employees. A nonkey employee, aged 60, is provided with $100,000 worth of coverage. Using the Uniform Premium Table I, the cost of $1,000 of protection per month in his age bracket is $.66. If the employee contributes $200 annually toward the cost of the coverage, what amount will be included in the employee's gross income?

    (A) $0
    (B) $196
    (C) $396
    (D) $792

11. Faith Forrester has the following selected information concerning her interest expenses and investment income for this year:

| | | |
|---|---|---|
| Interest income from corporate bonds | = | $5,000 |
| Dividend income not eligible for the lower maximum tax rates on qualifying dividends | = | $10,000 |
| Interest paid to acquire common stock portfolio | = | $18,000 |
| Interest income from public-purpose municipal bonds | = | $4,000 |
| Interest paid to acquire the municipal bonds | = | $2,000 |
| Qualified residence interest paid on principal residence | = | $10,000 |

    Based on the above information, the total amount of all of Faith's interest deductions for this year is

    (A) $15,000
    (B) $25,000
    (C) $28,000
    (D) $29,000

12. The Magic Missile Corporation has two shareholders. Past earnings and profits totaled $100,000. This year the corporation had earnings and profits of $200,000 and distributed $175,000 to each shareholder. How much of the distribution is taxable as a dividend to each shareholder?

    (A) $0
    (B) $100,000
    (C) $150,000
    (D) $175,000

13. Sally Snow is the beneficiary of her husband's $120,000 life insurance policy. Sally's husband died in September 2000. She elected to receive $7,800 annually under a life income option. Her life expectancy was 20 years when the life income option was chosen. How much of each annual annuity payment is included in her gross income?

    (A) $1,800
    (B) $3,800
    (C) $6,000
    (D) $7,800

14. Which of the following statements concerning the deductibility of bad debts is correct?

    (A) If a father guarantees his daughter's bank loan and she defaults, the father is entitled to a business bad-debt deduction.
    (B) Under certain circumstances a bad-debt deduction may be available even if a legal debt does not exist.
    (C) No deduction for partial worthlessness of a debt is allowed.
    (D) A nonbusiness bad debt can be deductible only as a short-term capital loss.

15. In order to be treated as a "qualifying child" of the taxpayer for dependency exemption purposes, an individual must generally meet which of the following tests?

    (A) The individual's gross income for the year must be less than the amount of the personal exemption.
    (B) The individual must have the same principal place of abode as the taxpayer for more than half of the taxable year.
    (C) The individual must be under the age of 17.
    (D) The taxpayer must provide 100 percent of the individual's support for the year.

16. Which of the following educational expenses would be deductible as a business expense by an individual taxpayer?

    (A) A practicing attorney pays for medical school because she wants to run for the office of city coroner.
    (B) A filing clerk pays for a night course in computer-based filing because his supervisor suggested he learn the more modern system since the office will be converting to it soon.
    (C) A carpenter pays for courses leading to a master's degree in literature to further broaden his horizons.
    (D) A salesman pays for courses in an MBA program to be qualified to apply for a job as vice president of finance.

17. Which of the following statements concerning the rules for taxation of capital gains for individual taxpayers is correct?

    (A) The current required holding period for long-term capital gains is more than 24 months.
    (B) Gain from the sale of collectibles is taxed at a maximum rate of 20 percent.
    (C) There must generally be a sale or exchange of a capital asset in order for the capital gain or loss rules to apply.
    (D) Short-term capital gains are taxed at a maximum rate of 28 percent.

18. This year Joe Carlton gave rental real estate worth $50,000 to his daughter Susan as a wedding present. Joe's adjusted basis in the property was $10,000. After Susan received the property, it generated $5,000 in income this year. Which of the following amounts will Susan have to include as income this year?

(A) $0
(B) $5,000
(C) $10,000
(D) $55,000

19. How many personal exemptions is a blind, unmarried taxpayer, aged 65 or older, who is not subject to the exemption phaseout rules, entitled to?

(A) The taxpayer is not entitled to any personal exemptions.
(B) The taxpayer is entitled to one personal exemption.
(C) The taxpayer is entitled to two personal exemptions.
(D) The taxpayer is entitled to three personal exemptions.

20. An executive bought 100 shares of his employer's stock for $2,000 on July 1 of this year. These shares are nontransferable and he must return them if he leaves the corporation. However, for each year he remains, 20 shares do not have to be returned. If the fair market value is $40 per share on July 1 of next year, the executive will have ordinary income next year of

(A) $400
(B) $800
(C) $2,000
(D) $4,000

21. For the current year an individual taxpayer age 70 will have the following income and medical expenses:
    Adjusted gross income = $100,000
    Medical expense insurance = $3,000
    Unreimbursed hospital and doctor bills = $2,000
    Unreimbursed prescription drug expenses = $1,000
The individual taxpayer will have a medical expense deduction for the current year of

(A) $0
(B) $1,000
(C) $3,000
(D) $6,000

22. A C corporation in the manufacturing business having $50,000 of taxable income for the year will pay federal income taxes in the amount of

(A) $7,500
(B) $12,500
(C) $17,000
(D) $19,500

23. Robert and Susan were just divorced. In accordance with the decree, he is paying her $1,000 per month as alimony and $600 per month for support of their twins, aged 5. How much of each monthly payment of $1,600 is allowed as a deduction from Robert's gross income?

   (A) $0
   (B) $600
   (C) $1,000
   (D) $1,600

24. An independent sales representative purchased a business car 3 years ago for $12,000. This year he exchanged the old business car now worth $6,000 with an adjusted basis of $5,000 plus $5,000 cash for a new business car with a selling price of $11,000. As a result of this exchange the sales representative recognized

   (A) no gain or loss
   (B) a $1,000 gain
   (C) a $6,000 loss
   (D) a $5,000 gain

25. In which of the following courts may a taxpayer petition for redetermination of an assessed income tax deficiency and receive a jury trial?

   (A) U.S. District Court
   (B) Court of Appeals for the Federal Circuit
   (C) U.S. Court of Federal Claims
   (D) U.S. Tax Court

26. Which of the following types of income would increase the exposure of a taxpayer to the 3.8 percent tax on net investment income?

   (A) interest income from an asset held in a trade or business
   (B) income from a qualified charitable remainder annuity trust or unitrust
   (C) capital gains from an asset not held in a trade or business
   (D) tax-exempt income

27. An individual taxpayer received an inheritance of $20,000 in cash, which he donated to a public charity. His adjusted gross income for the year is $30,000. The maximum charitable deduction that the taxpayer will be allowed for the current year is

   (A) $3,000
   (B) $9,000
   (C) $15,000
   (D) $20,000

28. In determining his individual income tax, each partner reports his distributive share of the partnership income. Subject to certain restrictions, a partner's distributive share is generally determined by

   (A) the current value of the capital account of each partner
   (B) the partnership agreement
   (C) the amount of salary payments made to a partner for services rendered
   (D) reference to the basis of each individual partner's interest

29. This year an individual taxpayer (other than a married individual filing a separate return) has $30,000 of investment interest expense and $1,000 of net investment income. The maximum amount of investment interest expense this taxpayer may deduct this year is

   (A) $0
   (B) $1,000
   (C) $10,000
   (D) $30,000

30. Which of the following statements correctly describes the option available to an annuitant if, in a given year, the annual payment from a variable annuity is $400 less than the annuitant's annual excludible amount?

   (A) The annuitant may use the $400 difference to offset other taxable income for the year in which the above annuity payment was received.
   (B) The annuitant may use the $400 difference to reduce his investment in the contract in the year following the one in which the above annuity payment was received.
   (C) The annuitant may recalculate his exclusion ratio for tax purposes for the year in which the above annuity payment was received.
   (D) The annuitant may recalculate his excludible amount beginning with payments to be received in the year following the one in which the above annuity payment was received.

31. A woman purchased a $100,000 whole life insurance policy on her life and designated her husband as beneficiary. Several years later the woman surrendered the policy for its cash value of $50,000. At the time of surrender, the woman had paid gross premiums of $45,000 and had received policy dividends of $10,000. What were the income tax consequences to the woman upon receipt of the cash surrender value?

   (A) She received the entire $50,000 tax free.
   (B) She received $45,000 tax free and $5,000 as ordinary income.
   (C) She received $35,000 tax free and $15,000 as ordinary income.
   (D) She received $15,000 tax free and $35,000 as ordinary income.

32. Which of the following statements concerning the exclusion of gain on the sale of a principal residence is correct?

   (A) The taxpayer must have occupied the residence for an aggregate of 4 out of the previous 5 years to be eligible for the exclusion.
   (B) The maximum exclusion for married couples filing jointly is $1 million.
   (C) There is no requirement that the taxpayer purchase a replacement residence to be eligible for the exclusion.
   (D) The maximum exclusion for single taxpayers is $500,000.

33. A corporation purchased a $50,000 whole life insurance policy on a man who was a key employee. Several years later the man terminated employment and his wife purchased the policy from the corporation with her own funds for $10,000. The wife designated herself as beneficiary and started paying the premiums. If the man were to die after his wife had paid net premiums amounting to $5,000, what would be the income tax consequences to the wife upon receipt of the policy death proceeds?

    (A) She would receive the entire $50,000 tax free.
    (B) She would receive $15,000 tax free and $35,000 as ordinary income.
    (C) She would receive $10,000 tax free and $40,000 as ordinary income.
    (D) She would receive the entire $50,000 as ordinary income.

34. The alternative minimum tax (AMT) is imposed on alternative minimum taxable income (AMTI) in excess of any applicable exemption amount. What tax rate is applied to the first $179,500 of the AMT base (or tentative minimum taxable income) of individual taxpayers?

    (A) 15 percent
    (B) 20 percent
    (C) 26 percent
    (D) 28 percent

35. Ben and John formed a corporation. John transferred $60,000 in cash to the corporation. Ben transferred property with a basis of $30,000 and a fair market value of $80,000. The corporation paid him $20,000 in cash. They each received back 50 percent of the stock of the corporation. How much gain will Ben recognize?

    (A) $20,000
    (B) $30,000
    (C) $60,000
    (D) $80,000

36. Which of the following statements concerning the deductibility of business expenses is (are) correct?

    I. Entertainment expenses are fully deductible if recorded by the taxpayer when incurred.
    II. Fines for the violation of a state law are deductible if they are incurred in the ordinary course of business.

    (A) I only
    (B) II only
    (C) Both I and II
    (D) Neither I nor II

37. Which of the following statements concerning dividends from a corporation to its shareholders is (are) correct?

    I. Cash dividends are generally taxed at a maximum rate of 20 percent under current law.
    II. Dividends of property other than money are considered capital transactions for income tax purposes.

(A) I only
(B) II only
(C) Both I and II
(D) Neither I nor II

38. Under which of the following circumstances will a corporation's payment of premiums on a life insurance policy be taxable to an insured employee?

    I. The corporation purchases group term life insurance of $10,000 payable to the insured employee's personal beneficiary under a nondiscriminatory plan.
    II. The insured employee is the owner of an individual policy and the proceeds are payable to the employee's personal beneficiary.

(A) I only
(B) II only
(C) Both I and II
(D) Neither I nor II

39. Which of the following statements concerning the tax implications of a divorce is (are) correct?

    I. Excess alimony payments are fully taxable to the recipient.
    II. Cash payments for child support provided in the divorce decree are tax deductible.

(A) I only
(B) II only
(C) Both I and II
(D) Neither I nor II

40. Which of the following statements correctly describe(s) a function of the federal income tax system?

    I. It can be used to reduce inflationary trends.
    II. It can be used to encourage economic activity at the taxpayer level.

(A) I only
(B) II only
(C) Both I and II
(D) Neither I nor II

41. Which of the following statements concerning S corporations is (are) correct?

    I. An S corporation may have only two classes of stock-preferred and common.
   II. The electing corporation must be a domestic corporation with no more than 50 shareholders.

    (A) I only
    (B) II only
    (C) Both I and II
    (D) Neither I nor II

42. Which of the following statements concerning sources of tax law is (are) correct?

    I. The IRS is bound to follow a decision of the Tax Court in subsequent cases involving the same issue.
   II. A two-thirds majority of both houses of Congress is needed to override the President's veto of a tax bill.

    (A) I only
    (B) II only
    (C) Both I and II
    (D) Neither I nor II

43. Which of the following statements concerning the small corporation exemption under the alternative minimum tax is (are) correct?

    I. To qualify for the exemption, the corporation must have no more than five shareholders.
   II. To qualify for the exemption, a new corporation must have average annual gross receipts of $5 million or less for its first 3 taxable years.

    (A) I only
    (B) II only
    (C) Both I and II
    (D) Neither I nor II

44. Which of the following items would be considered constructively received in the current year by a cash-basis taxpayer?

    I. interest earned from reinvestment of insurance policy dividends that are left with the insurance company
   II. income from work performed that has been billed but will not be received until next year

    (A) I only
    (B) II only
    (C) Both I and II
    (D) Neither I nor II

45. Which of the following statements concerning the itemized deduction for medical expenses is (are) correct?

    I. Any expenses for cosmetic surgery will qualify for the medical expense deduction.
    II. Physicians' fees are deductible at 50 percent of the cost.

    (A) I only
    (B) II only
    (C) Both I and II
    (D) Neither I nor II

46. Which of the following statements concerning capital cost recovery (depreciation) for assets placed in service this year is (are) correct?

    I. When the tax law specifies a particular type of depreciation method such as 150 percent declining balance, the taxpayer is precluded from using the straight-line method for that class of property.
    II. Automobiles are depreciated over a 3-year recovery period.

    (A) I only
    (B) II only
    (C) Both I and II
    (D) Neither I nor II

47. Which of the following statements concerning taxation of an annuity purchased this year is (are) correct?

    I. A portion of annuity payments received will be tax free as a return of capital for as long as the annuitant lives, regardless of how long.
    II. A gift of an annuity contract can result in a taxable event for the donor at the time of the gift.

    (A) I only
    (B) II only
    (C) Both I and II
    (D) Neither I nor II

48. Which of the following statements concerning the retirement of a general partner in a service partnership is (are) correct?

    I. Payments attributed to inventory and unrealized receivables will be treated as ordinary income to the retiring partner.
    II. Payment for goodwill will be treated as capital gain to the retiring partner if the partnership agreement provides for payments for goodwill.

    (A) I only
    (B) II only
    (C) Both I and II
    (D) Neither I nor II

49. Which of the following statements concerning the income tax treatment of disability income insurance benefits is (are) correct?

I. Benefits received from policies paid for by an employer are generally included in the employee's gross income.
II. Benefits from policies owned and paid for by the insured are taxable income to him or her when received.

(A) I only
(B) II only
(C) Both I and II
(D) Neither I nor II

50. Which of the following legal expenses of an individual taxpayer is (are) deductible in full for a single tax year as a nonbusiness expense?

I. legal expenses paid or incurred in connection with being represented at a tax audit
II. legal expenses paid or incurred in defending or perfecting title to real property

(A) I only
(B) II only
(C) Both I and II
(D) Neither I nor II

51. At the time of occurrence, which of the following events will require recognition of $1,000 of gross income by the taxpayer?

I. The taxpayer receives $1,000 in cash from his mother for his birthday.
II. A creditor cancels the taxpayer's debt of $1,000.

(A) I only
(B) II only
(C) Both I and II
(D) Neither I nor II

52. Which of the following statements concerning the income taxation of corporations is (are) correct?

I. Any corporation can fully deduct the dividends it receives each year from other corporations.
II. A corporation can only use capital losses to offset capital gains.

(A) I only
(B) II only
(C) Both I and II
(D) Neither I nor II

53. Which of the following statements concerning the doctrine of constructive receipt is (are) correct?

    I. The taxpayer has constructively received income when it is credited to his account without restrictions.
    II. It is inapplicable to individual taxpayers who report income on a cash basis.

(A) I only
(B) II only
(C) Both I and II
(D) Neither I nor II

54. A shareholder sells a portion of his stock in a corporation that he purchased at various prices and times. In this situation, which of the following statements concerning the method he may use to determine the basis of these shares is (are) correct?

    I. If he can adequately identify the shares sold, he can use the basis of those specific shares.
    II. If he is unable to identify the shares sold, he must use a "first-in, first-out" (FIFO) method to determine the basis.

(A) I only
(B) II only
(C) Both I and II
(D) Neither I nor II

55. A corporation pays the premiums on a life insurance policy on the life of its president. In which of the following situations may the corporation deduct the premiums as an expense?

    I. The corporation is the absolute owner and beneficiary of the policy.
    II. The president is the absolute owner of all rights under the policy and the corporation makes the premium payments pursuant to the president's compensation package.

(A) I only
(B) II only
(C) Both I and II
(D) Neither I nor II

56. Which of the following statements concerning the tax credit for qualified adoption expenses is (are) correct?

    I. The allowable amount of the credit is phased out for taxpayers whose adjusted gross income exceeds a specified amount.
    II. In the case of a foreign adoption, the credit is not allowable until the year in which the adoption becomes final.

(A) I only
(B) II only
(C) Both I and II
(D) Neither I nor II

57. Which of the following statements concerning the income tax treatment of qualified long-term care insurance contracts is (are) correct?

    I.  Premiums paid for such contracts are deductible as medical expenses subject to annual limitations based on the covered individual's age.

    II.  Premiums paid for such contracts are not eligible for the "above-the-line" deduction for health insurance premiums of self-employed taxpayers.

(A) I only
(B) II only
(C) Both I and II
(D) Neither I nor II

58. A newly formed corporation will have gross income in the current taxable year of $100,000. Which of the following would be fully deductible by the corporation for the current taxable year?

    I.  All of the organizational expenses incurred in forming the corporation

    II.  the payment of common stock dividends out of current earnings and profits

(A) I only
(B) II only
(C) Both I and II
(D) Neither I nor II

59. An individual taxpayer irrevocably assigns a level premium whole life insurance policy on his life to a qualified public charity. Which of the following statements concerning the charitable contribution deduction treatment of this policy gift is (are) correct?

    I.  The taxpayer will receive a charitable deduction in the current year equal to the lesser of the premiums paid or the value of the policy.

    II.  The taxpayer will receive a charitable deduction in the year of his death equal to the net policy proceeds.

(A) I only
(B) II only
(C) Both I and II
(D) Neither I nor II

60. Which of the following transactions between a corporation and its shareholders could result in a taxable distribution to the shareholders?

    I.  The corporation sells property to the shareholders at a price equivalent to the fair market value.

    II.  The corporation cancels debts that several shareholders owed to it.

(A) I only
(B) II only
(C) Both I and II
(D) Neither I nor II

61. A U.S. Supreme Court interpretation of tax law is the law of the land until which of the following happen(s)?

   I. Congress enacts a new statute, tantamount to overturning a Court decision.
   II. The Court overrides its own prior decision.

   (A) I only
   (B) II only
   (C) Both I and II
   (D) Neither I nor II

62. Which of the following statements concerning the personal-holding-company tax is (are) correct?

   I. One requirement to be treated as a personal holding company is that more than 50 percent of the value of the company's stock must be held by five or fewer individuals.
   II. The personal-holding-company tax can be avoided by the payment of dividends by the company.

   (A) I only
   (B) II only
   (C) Both I and II
   (D) Neither I nor II

63. Which of the following is (are) included in the gross income of an individual taxpayer?

   I. damages (other than punitive damages) received on account of a physical personal injury suffered by the taxpayer
   II. property received by the taxpayer as an inheritance

   (A) I only
   (B) II only
   (C) Both I and II
   (D) Neither I nor II

64. Which of the following statements concerning the limitations on passive activity losses is (are) correct?

   I. The limitations are generally designed to limit tax benefits with respect to activities in which the taxpayer does not materially participate.
   II. Excess passive losses disallowed under the limitations are allowed in the year the taxpayer disposes of his or her entire interest in the passive activity in a taxable disposition.

   (A) I only
   (B) II only
   (C) Both I and II
   (D) Neither I nor II

65. To substantiate entertainment deductions for business purposes, a record must be kept of which of the following?

    I. the business relationship to the taxpayer of the person entertained
    II. the date and place of the entertainment

(A) I only
(B) II only
(C) Both I and II
(D) Neither I nor II

66. A shareholder must meet which of the following requirements to avoid having the family attribution rules applied to an IRC Sec. 302 complete redemption?

    I. The shareholder must receive the proceeds in cash at the time the stock is redeemed by the corporation.
    II. The shareholder must repay all debts owed to the corporation at the time the stock is redeemed by the corporation.

(A) I only
(B) II only
(C) Both I and II
(D) Neither I nor II

67. Which of the following statements concerning stock redemptions under IRC Sec. 303 is (are) correct?

    I. The value of the stock used to qualify for a Sec. 303 redemption must generally exceed 35 percent of the decedent's adjusted gross estate.
    II. The proceeds of a stock redemption under Sec. 303 will be treated as a dividend for income tax purposes.

(A) I only
(B) II only
(C) Both I and II
(D) Neither I nor II

## READ THE FOLLOWING DIRECTIONS BEFORE CONTINUING

The questions below differ from the preceding questions in that they all contain the word EXCEPT. So you understand fully the basis used in selecting each answer, be sure to read each question carefully.

---

68. All the following requirements must be met for a corporation to obtain a deduction for payment of its president's salary EXCEPT

(A) The expense must be ordinary and necessary.
(B) The expense must generally be paid or incurred during the corporation's taxable year.
(C) The expense must be incurred in carrying on a trade or business.
(D) The expense must be directly attributable to the president's employment within the United States or its territories.

69. All the following statements concerning the tax credit for children are correct EXCEPT

   (A)  The amount of the credit is currently $1,000 per child.
   (B)  The credit is phased out for upper-income taxpayers.
   (C)  The taxpayer must be entitled to claim a dependency exemption for the child with respect to whom the credit is claimed.
   (D)  The credit is available with respect to children under the age of 21.

70. An individual may typically deduct all the following expenses from adjusted gross income EXCEPT

   (A)  state and local income taxes
   (B)  the attorney's fee for drafting a simple will
   (C)  state and local personal property taxes
   (D)  interest expense for a mortgage loan on his or her principal residence

71. All the following statements concerning the accumulated-earnings tax are correct EXCEPT

   (A)  It applies to accumulated earnings and profits retained by a corporation that are in excess of a specified amount and for which there is no reasonable business purpose.
   (B)  Its purpose is to prevent corporations from being used as devices to avoid personal income tax through the accumulation of corporate earnings.
   (C)  Retention of earnings to purchase key person insurance is generally considered a reasonable need of the business.
   (D)  Accumulations of $350,000 or less will automatically be considered as held for the reasonable needs of the business.

72. All the following statements concerning personal and dependency exemptions are correct EXCEPT

   (A)  A person who is the dependent of another taxpayer may not claim a personal exemption on his or her own return.
   (B)  Married taxpayers filing jointly are allowed a personal exemption for each spouse.
   (C)  Personal and dependency exemptions are subject to a phaseout for all taxpayers for the 2011 and 2012 tax years.
   (D)  In order to be claimed as a dependent under the dependency exemption rules, the dependent person must generally not file a joint return with his or her spouse.

73. All the following transfers by sale of a life insurance policy are excluded from the transfer-for-value rules EXCEPT

   (A)  sale of the policy to the insured
   (B)  sale of the policy to a partner of the insured
   (C)  sale of the policy to a corporation in which the insured is a shareholder
   (D)  sale of the policy to a shareholder in a corporation in which the insured is also a shareholder

74. All the following statements concerning benefits paid from dependent care assistance programs are correct EXCEPT

(A) The annual dollar limit on excludible benefits for married taxpayers filing jointly is $10,000.

(B) The amount excludible from gross income cannot exceed the earned income of the taxpayer for the year.

(C) To fully qualify for the income tax exclusion, the plan must meet certain nondiscrimination requirements.

(D) A payment to the employee's child under age 19 may not be excluded from the employee's gross income.

75. All the following kinds of property used in a trade or business or held for the production of income are depreciable or amortizable for tax purposes EXCEPT

(A) welding equipment

(B) rental apartment buildings

(C) automobiles

(D) land

76. All the following statements concerning the tax consequences of forming a partnership are correct EXCEPT

(A) As a general rule no gain or loss is recognized on the transfer of property or money to a partnership in exchange for a partnership interest.

(B) A partnership's basis in contributed property is the property's fair market value at the time of the transfer.

(C) The contributing partner's basis with respect to contributed property subject to indebtedness is reduced to the extent the indebtedness is taken over by the other partners.

(D) When a partner receives a partnership interest in exchange for services, the value of the interest may be taxable to the partner as compensation.

77. All the following statements concerning like-kind exchanges of property are correct EXCEPT

(A) A business may exchange real estate for a truck without recognition of gain or loss.

(B) Recognition of gain or loss in a like-kind exchange is postponed to a future taxable sale or exchange.

(C) In a like-kind exchange, gain is recognized to the extent of boot received in the exchange.

(D) A typical nontaxable exchange is one where a taxpayer trades in his or her old business truck plus cash for a new business truck.

78. All the following statements concerning the deductibility of casualty losses are correct EXCEPT

(A) To be deductible, a casualty loss must arise from an identifiable event.

(B) For personal losses of individuals the amount deductible cannot be greater than the adjusted basis of the property.

(C) Individuals are generally allowed a deduction for mislaid property.

(D) A deduction for nonbusiness casualty losses covered by insurance is allowable only if a timely claim had been filed with the insurer.

79. All the following statements concerning the alternative minimum tax (AMT) are correct EXCEPT

   (A) Interest on nongovernmental-purpose municipal bonds issued last year is considered a preference item for AMT purposes.
   (B) Each individual taxpayer has an exemption amount for AMT purposes that is unaffected by the amount of the taxpayer's AMTI.
   (C) The foreign tax credit may be used to offset the AMT.
   (D) Certain C corporations may be liable for AMT as a result of owning life insurance.

80. To determine adjusted gross income, all the following are potentially deductible, in whole or in part, from gross income EXCEPT

   (A) business expenses of self-employed taxpayers
   (B) charitable contributions of individuals
   (C) losses from the sale or exchange of property
   (D) alimony payments

81. Mrs. Morris sells all or some of her shares in the QT Corporation at a price in excess of her basis. The corporation has only one class of voting common stock. All the following qualify as capital transactions for Mrs. Morris EXCEPT

   (A) Mrs. Morris sells 25 percent of her shares to Mr. Smith, a stranger, in order to raise capital.
   (B) The QT Corporation redeems 200 of Mrs. Morris's 500 shares, and the remaining 500 outstanding shares are owned by her brother.
   (C) The corporation redeems all Mrs. Morris's shares in the corporation and none of the remaining shareholders is related to her.
   (D) The corporation redeems the shares that belong to Mrs. Morris, her son is the sole remaining stockholder, and she will be a director of QT.

82. All the following statements concerning the recovery periods and methods for determining cost recovery deductions for property placed in service this year are correct EXCEPT

   (A) There are prescribed recovery periods for all types of depreciable assets.
   (B) The applicable recovery periods for qualified recovery property range from 3 years to 39 years, depending on the type of property acquired.
   (C) The 5-year property class consists of tangible personal property, such as automobiles.
   (D) The depreciation method applicable to all property is the double-declining-balance method.

83. All the following statements concerning the income tax treatment of benefits received by an employee under an employer-financed nondiscriminatory accident and health plan are correct EXCEPT

   (A) Medical expense reimbursement benefits paid directly by the employer to the employee are excludible from the employee's gross income.
   (B) Benefits received in excess of the amount of expenses actually incurred for medical treatment are excludible from the employee's gross income.
   (C) Medical expense reimbursement benefits paid through an insurance company are excludible from the employee's gross income.
   (D) Benefits received for permanent disfigurement in an amount computed without regard to the period the employee is away from work are excludible from the employee's gross income.

84. All the following statements concerning the income tax status of a family partnership are correct EXCEPT

   (A) The IRS may ignore the partnership agreement and reallocate income for tax purposes to properly reflect the economic reality of the partnership arrangement.
   (B) A family partnership is generally structured to shift income within the family so that the total income taxes of family members are less than if the business were a sole proprietorship.
   (C) If a family member is to be considered a partner in a family partnership in which capital is a material income-producing factor, the family member must have acquired his capital interest through a bona fide transaction.
   (D) Without contributing services to the partnership, a family member can be treated as a partner in a family partnership whose income consists primarily of fees or commissions.

85. Individual taxpayers can deduct all the following types of losses EXCEPT

   (A) losses incurred in a trade or business
   (B) losses incurred in a transaction entered into for profit
   (C) personal losses that arise from a fire, storm, shipwreck, or other casualty, or from a theft
   (D) personal losses that arise from the gradual wearing out of property held for personal use

86. All the following statements concerning the deductibility of various expenses in connection with a taxpayer's trade or business are correct EXCEPT

   (A) Living expenses at a temporary residence while away from home for 6 months are generally deductible.
   (B) Deductions for bribes paid to public officials are disallowed.
   (C) The expenses of commuting are deductible if the taxpayer lives more than 50 miles away from his place of business.
   (D) A bonus paid to an employee is subject to the same test of reasonableness applicable to other salary payments in determining its deductibility.

87. An individual sold his interest in a partnership to another individual. All the following statements concerning the income taxation of the sale proceeds to the individual are correct EXCEPT

(A) That portion of the proceeds which represents his share of the potential gain on partnership inventory is taxable to him as ordinary income.

(B) That portion of the proceeds which represents specified goodwill is taxable to him as a capital gain.

(C) That portion of the proceeds which represents his share of depreciable partnership property with a fair market value in excess of basis is received by him on a tax-free basis.

(D) That portion of the proceeds which represents his share of unrealized receivables is taxable to him as ordinary income.

88. All of the following statements concerning the Hope scholarship and American opportunity credits for higher education expenses are correct EXCEPT

(A) To claim the credit, the student on whose behalf the expenses are paid must be at least a "half-time" student.

(B) The credit cannot be claimed with respect to the same expenses for which the taxpayer elects to claim the Lifetime learning credit.

(C) The credit is phased out for taxpayers with modified adjusted gross income above specified levels.

(D) A credit of up to $5,000 per year may be claimed with respect to the expenses of each eligible student.

89. All the following are considered to be nondeductible personal, living, or family expenses EXCEPT

(A) rent, water, and utility payments made by the taxpayer on his residence

(B) life insurance premiums paid by the taxpayer on the life of his mother

(C) interest on a $250,000 first mortgage secured by the taxpayer's residence

(D) fire and casualty insurance premiums for the taxpayer's residence

90. All the following statements concerning the calculation of an individual taxpayer's alternative minimum taxable income (AMTI) are correct EXCEPT

(A) State and local taxes deducted in determining the regular income tax are added back to taxable income in calculating AMTI.

(B) Charitable contributions deducted in determining the regular income tax are added back to taxable income in calculating AMTI.

(C) Personal and dependency exemptions are added back to taxable income in calculating AMTI.

(D) The standard deduction is added back to taxable income in calculating AMTI if the taxpayer uses the standard deduction.

91. All the following taxes may generally be deducted by an individual taxpayer who itemizes his deductions EXCEPT

(A) state income taxes

(B) local real property taxes

(C) federal income taxes

(D) local income taxes

92. All the following statements concerning the attribution rules for determining constructive ownership of stock are correct EXCEPT

  (A) Shares of stock owned by a father are considered as being owned by his daughter's husband.
  (B) Shares of stock owned by an estate are considered as being owned proportionately by its beneficiaries having a direct present interest in the estate.
  (C) Shares of stock owned by a trust are considered as being owned by its beneficiaries in proportion to their actuarial interests in the trust.
  (D) Shares of stock owned by a partnership are considered as being owned proportionately by the partners.

93. All the following statements concerning IRS revenue rulings are correct EXCEPT

  (A) They are issued when the IRS wishes to resolve unclear points of law.
  (B) They have the force and effect of law and must be followed by the courts.
  (C) They are issued if a stated set of facts involving a problem common to many taxpayers is recognized.
  (D) They are binding on IRS revenue agents in their handling of issues in current taxpayer cases.

94. Julie is a partner in a partnership. All the following statements concerning adjustments to Julie's interest in the partnership are correct EXCEPT

  (A) Basis is decreased by Julie's share of the partnership's liability to her to the extent that she loaned money to the partnership as an outsider.
  (B) Basis is decreased by distributions made to Julie.
  (C) Basis is decreased by Julie's share of any partnership losses.
  (D) Basis is increased by Julie's share of increased partnership liabilities.

95. All the following statements concerning the tax aspects of withdrawals from universal life policies are correct EXCEPT

  (A) Withdrawals will be taxable only if the policy is a modified endowment contract (MEC).
  (B) Withdrawals associated with a reduction in the policy's death benefit may be subject to "last-in, first-out" (LIFO) tax treatment.
  (C) Special rules apply to withdrawals occurring during the first 15 policy years.
  (D) Withdrawals during the first 5 policy years may have a higher taxable portion than withdrawals made during years 6 through 15.

96. All the following statements concerning the private rulings issued by the IRS are correct EXCEPT

  (A) They are published and made available to the public.
  (B) They are issued at the request of an individual taxpayer.
  (C) They are binding upon the IRS only for the particular case in point.
  (D) They can be used as precedents by taxpayers in general.

97. All the following statements concerning the time for filing tax returns are correct EXCEPT

(A) Individual tax returns are generally due on or before April 15 of the year following a given tax year.
(B) An automatic extension can be obtained by individuals by filing Form 4868 on or before the due date.
(C) Some corporations may have a tax year that operates on a 12-month period beginning on a day other than January 1.
(D) A corporation's tax return is generally due on the fifteenth day of the fourth month following the close of the tax year.

98. All the following statements concerning the use of life insurance in the context of a divorce settlement are correct EXCEPT

(A) An existing cash value policy transferred by one spouse to the other results in taxable income to the recipient spouse.
(B) If one spouse owns a policy and the other spouse pays the premiums after the divorce, the premium payments are generally treated as alimony.
(C) If one spouse owns the policy, pays the premiums, and names the other spouse as beneficiary, the premiums are not deductible.
(D) Death benefits paid under policies used in divorce settlements will generally be free of income tax.

99. All the following are basic requirements for the allowance of a depreciation deduction EXCEPT

(A) the taxpayer generally must have an ownership interest in the asset
(B) the asset's useful life must be limited
(C) the asset must be used only in the taxpayer's trade or business
(D) the taxpayer must have a tax basis in the asset

100. All the following statements concerning the alternative minimum tax (AMT) are correct EXCEPT

(A) Medical expenses in excess of 7.5 percent of adjusted gross income are deductible in computing alternative minimum taxable income.
(B) The AMT is imposed upon certain corporations at a rate of 20 percent.
(C) The adoption credit is allowable in computing AMT liability.
(D) The AMT is imposed only if it exceeds the taxpayer's regular income tax.

# Answer Key for *Income Taxation* Sample Examination

| Question Number | Correct Answer | Chapter | Question Number | Correct Answer | Chapter |
|:---:|:---:|:---:|:---:|:---:|:---:|
| 1 | C | 20 | 51 | B | 3 |
| 2 | B | 14 | 52 | B | 18 |
| 3 | A | 13 | 53 | A | 3 |
| 4 | C | 11 | 54 | C | 13 |
| 5 | B | 9 | 55 | B | 16 |
| 6 | C | 6 | 56 | C | 10 |
| 7 | D | 4 | 57 | A | 9 |
| 8 | A | 7 | 58 | D | 18 |
| 9 | B | 2 | 59 | A | 9 |
| 10 | B | 5 | 60 | B | 19 |
| 11 | B | 9 | 61 | C | 2 |
| 12 | C | 19 | 62 | C | 18 |
| 13 | A | 16 | 63 | D | 6 |
| 14 | D | 8 | 64 | C | 12 |
| 15 | B | 4 | 65 | C | 7 |
| 16 | B | 7 | 66 | D | 19 |
| 17 | C | 14 | 67 | A | 19 |
| 18 | B | 6 | 68 | D | 7 |
| 19 | B | 4 | 69 | D | 10 |
| 20 | A | 5 | 70 | B | 9 |
| 21 | A | 9 | 71 | D | 18 |
| 22 | A | 18 | 72 | C | 4 |
| 23 | C | 5 | 73 | D | 16 |
| 24 | A | 13 | 74 | A | 6 |
| 25 | A | 2 | 75 | D | 11 |
| 26 | C | 14 | 76 | B | 20 |
| 27 | C | 9 | 77 | A | 13 |
| 28 | B | 20 | 78 | C | 8 |
| 29 | B | 9 | 79 | B | 15 |
| 30 | D | 5 | 80 | B | 4, 8 |
| 31 | C | 16 | 81 | D | 19 |
| 32 | C | 13 | 82 | D | 11 |
| 33 | B | 16 | 83 | B | 6 |
| 34 | C | 15 | 84 | D | 20 |
| 35 | A | 18 | 85 | D | 8 |
| 36 | D | 7 | 86 | C | 7 |
| 37 | A | 19 | 87 | C | 20 |

| Question Number | Correct Answer | Chapter | Question Number | Correct Answer | Chapter |
|---|---|---|---|---|---|
| 38 | B | 5, 16 | 88 | D | 10 |
| 39 | D | 5 | 89 | C | 9 |
| 40 | C | 2 | 90 | B | 15 |
| 41 | D | 18 | 91 | C | 9 |
| 42 | B | 2 | 92 | A | 19 |
| 43 | B | 15 | 93 | B | 2 |
| 44 | A | 3 | 94 | A | 20 |
| 45 | D | 9 | 95 | A | 16 |
| 46 | D | 11 | 96 | D | 2 |
| 47 | B | 5 | 97 | D | 4 |
| 48 | C | 20 | 98 | A | 5 |
| 49 | A | 6 | 99 | C | 11 |
| 50 | A | 7 | 100 | A | 15 |

# Explanation of Answers to *Income Taxation* Sample Examination

1. The answer is **(C)**.
   The distributive share of a partnership's operating loss that is deductible by an individual partner is limited to the adjusted basis of his or her partnership interest. Hence Smith's adjusted basis in his partnership interest is $40,000, determined by his adjusted basis for the property he has contributed.

2. The answer is **(B)**.
   (A) is incorrect because the maximum rate is generally 20 percent.
   (C) is incorrect because collectibles gain is subject to a 28 percent maximum rate.
   (D) is incorrect because such unrecaptured depreciation is subject to a 25 percent maximum rate.

3. The answer is **(A)**.
   The couple is eligible for the full $500,000 exclusion under the rules for married couples. Their realized gain is $450,000 ($650,000 – $200,000). Therefore, no gain is taxable.

4. The answer is **(C)**.
   (A) is incorrect because 5-year property is subject to a "half-year" convention.
   (B) is incorrect because the convention does apply in the year in which the property is disposed of.
   (D) is incorrect because real estate is generally subject to a "mid-month" convention.

5. The answer is **(B)**.
   Allowing a charitable, religious, educational, or similar organization to use property on a rent-free basis does not give rise to a charitable deduction.

6. The answer is **(C)**.
   Any gain from the sale of tax-exempt securities is subject to federal income taxation. Since the bonds are public-purpose bonds, the interest is tax exempt.

7. The answer is **(D)**.
   (A) is incorrect because the personal exemption amount is indexed for inflation.
   (B) is incorrect because the kiddie tax is applicable to the net unearned income of children under a specified age.
   (C) is incorrect because married taxpayers filing jointly receive the highest standard deduction amount.

8. The answer is **(A)**.
   The tuition for CLU courses is paid for the purpose of maintaining or improving skills necessary to the agent's current employment.
   (B) is incorrect because his primary office is not at home, and the basic cost of his first line is nondeductible.
   (C) is incorrect because personal insurance premiums are generally nondeductible.
   (D) is incorrect because commuting expenses are nondeductible.

9. The answer is **(B)**.
   The Tax Court is the only court that will hear a tax case without prior payment of the assessed deficiency.
   (A) is incorrect because there are no jury trials in the Court of Federal Claims.
   (C) is incorrect because prepayment of the assessed deficiency is required in the District Court.
   (D) is incorrect because the Tax Court does not have jury trials.

10. The answer is **(B)**.
    Premiums for the first $50,000 of coverage are tax free to the employee. The Table I cost for the excess coverage ($50,000) is taxable to the extent that it exceeds the employee's

contribution. Here, this Table I cost is $396 per year (.66 × 12 × 50). Therefore $196 is taxable to the employee ($396 − $200).

11. The answer is **(B)**.
Faith can deduct investment interest up to the limit of her net investment income. However, municipal bond interest income or the interest paid to acquire municipal bonds does not qualify as investment income or interest. Thus, the only investment interest that qualifies is the $18,000 paid to acquire the common stocks. Since Faith has only $15,000 of net investment income, she is limited to a $15,000 investment interest deduction. The $10,000 mortgage interest on the home is fully deductible. Faith has total interest deductions this year of $25,000.

12. The answer is **(C)**.
The distribution to each shareholder is taxed as a dividend to the extent of the pro rata earnings and profits of the corporation, both accumulated and current. The combined earnings and profits in this case totaled $300,000. Therefore $150,000 of the distribution to each of the two shareholders is a dividend.

13. The answer is **(A)**.
Under the settlement option chosen, Sally receives $7,800 annually; $6,000 represents the death benefit that is nontaxable to her. The remaining portion, $1,800, represents payment of interest, which is taxable as ordinary income.

14. The answer is **(D)**.
(A) is incorrect because in a family situation the guarantor of a loan is not acting in the course of his or her trade or business.
(B) is incorrect because a legal (enforceable) debt is a prerequisite to the deduction.
(C) is incorrect because a taxpayer may take a deduction for partial worthlessness if the debt is a business bad debt and the circumstances warrant it.

15. The answer is **(B)**.
(A) is incorrect because the gross income test applies for purposes of determining whether an individual is a "qualifying relative," not a "qualifying child."
(C) is incorrect because a qualifying child must generally be below the age of 19, not 17. (Different rules apply for full-time students and disabled individuals.)
(D) is incorrect because the support test for a qualifying child requires only that the individual not provide more than half of his or her own support.

16. The answer is **(B)**.
Educational expenses are deductible as business expenses if the education is to improve skills in the taxpayer's current job or is required by the taxpayer's employer. However, education leading to a career change does not give rise to a business expense deduction, even though a different tax deduction or credit might be available for the expense.

17. The answer is **(C)**.
In the case of capital assets, realization of gain or loss generally occurs through a sale or taxable exchange of the asset.

18. The answer is **(B)**.
Only the $5,000 of income generated by the gifted property is includible in Susan's gross income.

19. The answer is **(B)**.
Older or blind taxpayers receive an additional amount in the determination of their standard deduction. However, they do not receive additional personal exemptions.

20. The answer is **(A)**.

The executive has a basis of $20 per share ($2,000 ÷ 100). Their value when the restriction lapses is $40 per share. Therefore the executive has income of $20 per share ($40 – $20), for a total of $400 ($20 × 20 shares).

21. The answer is **(A)**.
The total medical expenses ($6,000) are less than the applicable percentage floor of adjusted gross income ($7,500 for taxpayers under 65 and $10,000 for taxpayers 65 and older).

22. The answer is **(A)**.
The 15 percent tax bracket applies to the first $50,000 of corporate taxable income. Therefore the tax is $7,500 ($50,000 × .15).

23. The answer is **(C)**.
Only the $1,000 alimony portion of Robert's payments is deductible.

24. The answer is **(A)**.
The taxpayer has realized no taxable gain on the exchange, so there is no recognized gain. The exchange would appear to qualify as a like-kind exchange even if gain were realized. Also, the taxpayer paid cash boot in the exchange, but did not receive boot that would cause the recognition of gain.

25. The answer is **(A)**.
The U.S. District Court is the only court in which a taxpayer can have a jury trial in a civil tax case.

26. The answer is **(C)**.
Capital gains from an asset not held in a trade or business is specifically included within the meaning of net investment income. The income described in (A), (B), and (D) is exempted from the meaning of net investment income.

27. The answer is **(C)**.
The current deduction is limited to one-half of adjusted gross income, or $15,000 in this case.

28. The answer is **(B)**.
Salary, capital accounts, and basis are not necessarily related to the partner's distributive share, which is determined under the partnership agreement.

29. The answer is **(B)**.
The deduction is limited to the taxpayer's net investment income for the year, or $1,000.

30. The answer is **(D)**.
In the case of a variable annuity, the annuitant may recalculate the exclusion ratio with respect to future payments if he or she receives a payment that is less than the currently excludible amount.

31. The answer is **(C)**.
The woman's basis in the policy is $35,000 ($45,000 premiums – $10,000 dividends received). Therefore the taxable amount is $15,000 ($50,000 received – $35,000 basis).

32. The answer is **(C)**.
(A) is incorrect because the occupancy requirement is 2 out of 5 years.
(B) is incorrect because the maximum exclusion is $500,000.
(D) is incorrect because the maximum exclusion for single taxpayers is $250,000.

33. The answer is **(B)**.
This is a transfer-for-value situation. The wife paid $10,000 for the policy and $5,000 in subsequent premiums, a total basis of $15,000. She must pay tax on the proceeds in excess of $15,000.

34. The answer is **(C)**.

The individual AMT rate is 26 percent on the first $179,500.

35. The answer is **(A)**.
When property is transferred in a tax-free incorporation, there is no recognition of gain or loss to the transferor if only stock is received in exchange. However, gain will be recognized to Ben to the extent of money or other property received ($20,000).

36. The answer is **(D)**.
I is incorrect because with few exceptions, only 50 percent of entertainment expenses are deductible.
II is incorrect because fines for violation of law are not deductible, even if they are incurred in the ordinary course of business.

37. The answer is **(A)**.
II is incorrect because a distribution of any type of property in the form of a dividend can be taxed as a dividend and not as a capital transaction.

38. The answer is **(B)**.
The insured employee is taxed on the coverage because the employee is the owner of the policy.
I is incorrect because the insurance premiums would not be taxable. These premiums will qualify for the exclusion under IRC Sec. 79.

39. The answer is **(D)**.
I is incorrect because the recipient of excess alimony payments receives a deduction for such payments in the third postseparation year.
II is incorrect because child support payments are not deductible.

40. The answer is **(C)**.
Both I and II are correct.

41. The answer is **(D)**.
I is incorrect because an S corporation may not have preferred stock. II is incorrect because an S corporation may have up to 100 shareholders.

42. The answer is **(B)**.
I is incorrect because the IRS is not bound to follow Tax Court decisions.

43. The answer is **(B)**.
I is incorrect because there is no requirement concerning the number of shareholders in the corporation.

44. The answer is **(A)**.
II is incorrect because a cash-basis taxpayer reports income when received, not when he or she has completed the work and submitted a bill for services.

45. The answer is **(D)**.
I is incorrect because expenses for cosmetic surgery are subject to strict rules regarding deductibility under current law.
II is incorrect because allowable medical expenses, including physicians' fees, are fully deductible as itemized deductions, but only to the extent that they exceed the applicable percent of the taxpayer's adjusted gross income.

46. The answer is **(D)**.
I is incorrect because the law permits taxpayers the option to elect straight-line depreciation for any asset class placed in service during the year.
II is incorrect because automobiles currently placed in service are depreciated over a 5-year recovery period.

47. The answer is **(B)**.

I is incorrect because the tax-free amount recoverable for an annuity purchased this year is limited to the individual's investment in the contract. Once the investment in the contract is fully recovered, the full amount of each annuity payment is taxable.

48. The answer is **(C)**.
Both I and II are correct.

49. The answer is **(A)**.
II is incorrect because benefits on disability policies personally owned and paid for by the insured are not taxable.

50. The answer is **(A)**.
II is incorrect because legal expenses paid to defend or perfect title to property are generally not deductible in full for a single tax year. Those legal expenses may be capitalized and will be recovered when the property is depreciated or sold.

51. The answer is **(B)**.
I is incorrect because the $1,000 in this situation is a gift, and gifts are not includible in the gross income of the recipient.

52. The answer is **(B)**.
I is incorrect because the dividends-received deduction, if available, is generally less than 100 percent.

53. The answer is **(A)**.
II is incorrect because the doctrine of constructive receipt applies specifically to cash-basis taxpayers.

54. The answer is **(C)**.
Both I and II are correct.

55. The answer is **(B)**.
I is incorrect because a corporation cannot deduct premiums paid on a policy if the corporation is a beneficiary.

56. The answer is **(C)**.
Both I and II are correct.

57. The answer is **(A)**.
II is incorrect because premiums for qualified long-term care insurance contracts are eligible for the "above-the-line" deduction.

58. The answer is **(D)**.
I is incorrect because organizational expenses in excess of the deductible limit permitted under section 195 of the Internal Revenue Code must be amortized over a 180-month period.
II is incorrect because dividends paid are not deductible regardless of the amount of the corporation's earnings and profits.

59. The answer is **(A)**.
II is incorrect because there is no income tax charitable deduction for policy proceeds. The deduction is taken in the year of contribution and is not based upon the death proceeds.

60. The answer is **(B)**.
I is incorrect because a sale of property at fair market value by a corporation to its shareholders is not treated as a dividend or other taxable distribution made with respect to stock ownership.

61. The answer is **(C)**.
Both I and II are correct.

62. The answer is **(C)**.
Both I and II are correct.

63. The answer is **(D)**.
I is incorrect because damages (other than punitive damages) received on account of a physical personal injury are generally not taxable.
II is incorrect because property received by inheritance is generally not taxable.

64. The answer is **(C)**.
Both I and II are correct.

65. The answer is **(C)**.
Both I and II are correct.

66. The answer is **(D)**.
I is incorrect because it is immaterial under the attribution rules whether the shareholder receives cash at the time of the redemption.
II is incorrect because there is no requirement that the shareholder repay debts to the corporation in order to avoid family attribution.

67. The answer is **(A)**.
II is incorrect because proceeds of a Sec. 303 redemption are treated as made in exchange for a capital asset and are therefore eligible for capital gains treatment.

68. The answer is **(D)**.
There is no requirement that salaries be earned within the United States or its territories.

69. The answer is **(D)**.
The credit is available with respect to children under age 17.

70. The answer is **(B)**.
While attorneys' fees are deductible as they relate to business, profit making, or tax matters, the drafting of a simple will is a personal expenditure that is nondeductible.

71. The answer is **(D)**.
The accumulated-earnings tax credit (or exemption) is $250,000 ($150,000 for professional service corporations).

72. The answer is **(C)**.
For 2011 and 2012, exemptions are not subject to a phaseout.

73. The answer is **(D)**.
This sale of a policy to another shareholder is not an exception to the transfer-for-value rules.

74. The answer is **(A)**.
The dollar limit is $5,000.

75. The answer is **(D)**.
Land may not be depreciated for tax purposes.

76. The answer is **(B)**.
A partnership generally retains the same basis in contributed property as the property had in the hands of the contributing partner.

77. The answer is **(A)**.
Real estate and trucks are not like-kind property under IRC Sec. 1031.

78. The answer is **(C)**.
Mislaid property generally does not give rise to a deductible loss.

79. The answer is **(B)**.
The amount of an individual taxpayer's exemption is reduced when a taxpayer's AMTI reaches a specified dollar amount.

80. The answer is **(B)**.

Charitable contributions are deductible, with certain limitations, from adjusted gross income (not gross income) in determining taxable income. The other expenses listed are deductible from gross income in determining adjusted gross income.

81. The answer is **(D)**.
Although the corporation redeems all of Mrs. Morris's shares, she is constructively deemed to own the shares belonging to her son and will therefore be denied capital transaction tax treatment on the redemption. She cannot claim a waiver of the family attribution rules because of her status as a director of QT Corporation.

82. The answer is **(D)**.
Only property in the 3-year, 5-year, 7-year, and 10-year classes can use the double-declining-balance method. Classes of 15 years and 20 years use 150 percent declining balance. Both residential and nonresidential real estate use the straight-line method.

83. The answer is **(B)**.
Benefits received in excess of medical expenses incurred will be includible in gross income.

84. The answer is **(D)**.
A family member in a partnership which is in the business of performing services must contribute services to the partnership to be treated as a partner for tax purposes.

85. The answer is **(D)**.
The wearing out of property held for personal use does not give rise to a tax deduction.

86. The answer is **(C)**.
Commuting expenses are nondeductible regardless of the distance involved.

87. The answer is **(C)**.
Proceeds received for the fair market value of property in excess of its basis are taxable.

88. The answer is **(D)**.
The maximum credit is subject to annual indexing adjustments for inflation, but is considerably less than $5,000.

89. The answer is **(C)**.
Interest on a first mortgage of up to $1 million of principal secured by the taxpayer's residence will generally qualify as deductible qualified residence interest.

90. The answer is **(B)**.
Charitable contributions are deductible in computing AMTI.

91. The answer is **(C)**.
Federal income taxes are not deductible.

92. The answer is **(A)**.
The attribution rules apply from parent to child and between spouses, but not from a parent to the spouse of a child because the family attribution rules cannot be applied twice in succession.

93. The answer is **(B)**.
The courts are not bound to follow revenue rulings, which represent only the position of the IRS on a given issue.

94. The answer is **(A)**.
Any liability to the partner by the partnership will increase, not decrease, basis.

95. The answer is **(A)**.
Withdrawals from such policies may be taxable even if the policy is not a MEC.

96. The answer is **(D)**.

Private rulings cannot be used as legal precedents.

97. The answer is **(D)**.
A corporation's return is generally due on the fifteenth day of the third month following the close of its tax year, not the fourth month.

98. The answer is **(A)**. Such a transfer will not result in a taxable event.

99. The answer is **(C)**.
Assets held for the production of income as well as assets used in a trade or business may qualify for depreciation deductions.

100. The answer is **(A)**.
The medical expense "floor" for AMT purposes is 10 percent for all taxpayers regardless of age at the close of the tax year.

# THE AMERICAN COLLEGE
# ALUMNI
# ASSOCIATION

Welcome! Membership in The Alumni Association is all about pride—in your education, industry and your affiliation with the best financial services education in the country.

Dedicated to lifelong learning, communications and recognition, The Alumni Association serves more than 38,000 members who take advantage of this free membership. Whether you are a current student, designee, or degree holder, you are entitled you to all these benefits:

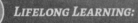

## *LIFELONG LEARNING:*

- **Thought provoking presentations** held across the country on topics that impact your practice.
- **Continuing education** opportunities that keep your credentials and expertise timely.

## *RECOGNITION:*

- **Awards** for professional success and exemplary volunteerism, including the Alumni Association Hall of Fame and Alumnus of the Month.
- **Building industry awareness** for your designations.
- **The Alumni Store** offers great products to showcase your College pride.
- **DesignationCheck.com** helps consumers find advisors near them with CLU®, ChFC®, or CFP® Certification designations.

*Among the numerous perks of being a graduate of The American College, belonging to the Alumni Association is one of the best. Experience all the great benefits the Alumni Association has to offer, including a free subscription to The Wealth Channel Magazine, as part of your free membership!*

Mickey Rosenzweig, CLU®, ChFC®, AEP
President, The American College
Alumni Association

## *COMMUNICATION:*

- **The Wealth Channel Magazine** is the nation's definitive source of insight and knowledge into the creation of financial security.
- **Connections Newsletter** provides you with monthly updates on the profession and The College.
- **News and updates** keep you up-to-date with your industry and your peers.

## *TRAVEL OPPORTUNITIES:*

- **Alumni Live Tours** bring the best of The College to cities all over the country.
- **Travel & Learn Cruises** take you to exotic destinations, provide memories to last a lifetime, and offer top-quality CE credits.
- **Knowledge Summit:** Attend career-boosting presentations and celebrate your achievement by walking at Commencement.

## *FIND US ONLINE!*

- **TheAmericanCollege.edu/Alumni**
- **Facebook.com/TheAmericanCollege**
- **Twitter.com/TheAmerCol**
- **TheAmericanCollege.edu/LinkedIn**

The American College • 270 South Bryn Mawr Avenue, Bryn Mawr, PA 19010 • 610-526-1477